# The Private Degas

Degas, *Self-portrait*, 1857. Etching and drypoint. 23 × 14.4 cms.
Williamstown, Mass., Sterling and Francine Clark Art Institute. CAT. 9

# The
# Private
# Degas

## Richard Thomson

## The Herbert Press

First published in Great Britain 1987 by
The Herbert Press Limited, 46 Northchurch Road, London N1 4EJ

Designer Pauline Harrison
House Editor Curigwen Lewis

Printed in Great Britain by Jolly & Barber Ltd, Rugby
Bound in Great Britain by Norton Bridge Bookbinders

British Library Cataloguing in Publication Data

Thomson, Richard, *1953* –

  The Private Degas
  1. Degas, Edgar——Criticism and
  interpretation
  I. Title
  759.4     ND553.D3

  ISBN 0–906969–67–0

Front cover illustration: Degas, *After the Bath*, *c.*1905. CAT. 103
Back cover illustration: Degas, *Race Horses*, *c.*1875–8. CAT. 50

# Contents

# Preface

While linked through exhibitions and in the public mind with the Impressionists, Degas dismissed any thought that his work derived from a spontaneous response to his subject. His was an art built, first, on study of the old masters and then on constant exploration, the working and reworking of themes, poses and compositions. *The Private Degas* began as a project about his drawing and expanded in ambition to relate his work as a draughtsman to that of the painter, sculptor and printmaker.

The exhibition and this book are the results of long and persistent research by Richard Thomson. His approach casts new light on the way Degas's art came about, and how 'the private Degas' relates to his more public face.

We are grateful to him and to the many generous owners of Degas's work whom he persuaded to lend in spite of the competing demands of recent and imminent Degas exhibitions elsewhere.

Appropriately the exhibition is being shown at the Whitworth Art Gallery in the University of Manchester, where Mr Thomson lectures in the history of art, and at the Fitzwilliam Museum in Cambridge, whose outstanding Degas collections are substantially represented here.

Joanna Drew
*Director of Art*

Michael Harrison
*Assistant Director for Regional Exhibitions*

# Acknowledgements

During the preparation of *The Private Degas* I have been provided with generous assistance and advice by many people, private collectors, dealers, fellow art historians, librarians, and museum curators. I am most grateful to them for their help, and offer them all my warmest thanks. In particular, I am indebted to Paul Tanner, Kunstmuseum Basel; Alexandra Murphy, Barbara Shapiro and Theodore Stebbins, Museum of Fine Arts, Boston; Dr Annemarie Winther, Kunsthalle Bremen; Craig Hartley, Jane Munro and David Scrase, Fitzwilliam Museum, Cambridge; Dr Konrad Oberhuber, Fogg Art Museum, Cambridge, Mass.; Dr Richard Brettell, Dr Douglas Druick, Suzanne Folds McCullagh and the late Harold Joachim, The Art Institute of Chicago; Edward Henning, Louise Richards and Evan Turner, The Cleveland Museum of Art; Patrice Marandel, The Detroit Institute of Arts; Michael Clarke, National Gallery of Scotland, Edinburgh; Philip Vainker, The Burrell Collection, Glasgow; Norma Johnson and Dr Norman Tennent, Glasgow Art Gallery; Erika Billeter, Musée Cantonal des Beaux-Arts, Lausanne; Frances Carey, Antony Griffiths and John Rowlands, Dept of Prints and Drawings, The British Museum, London; Professor Alan Bowness, The Tate Gallery, London; Professor C.R. Dodwell, Francis Hawcroft and Julian Tomlin, Whitworth Art Gallery, University of Manchester; Jacob Bean, Calvin Brown and Gary Tinterow, Metropolitan Museum, New York; Christopher Lloyd and Dr Nicholas Penny, Ashmolean Museum, Oxford; Roseline Bacou, Henri Loyrette and Geneviève Monnier, Paris, Musée du Louvre; A.W.F.M. Meij, Boymans-van Beuningen Museum, Rotterdam; Dr Ulrike Gauss, Staatsgalerie, Stuttgart; Roger Mandle, Toledo Museum of Art; Götz Adriani, Kunsthalle Tübingen; Beverly Carter, Paul Mellon Collection, Washington; Meg Grasselli and Carlotta Owens, National Gallery of Art, Washington; David Brooke and Rafael Fernandez, Sterling and Francine Clark Art Institute, Williamstown, Mass.

My thanks go also to William Acquavella, Acquavella Galleries, New York; Adrian Eeles, Artemis Fine Arts (UK) Ltd; David Ellis-Jones, Christie's; Marianne and Walter Feilchenfeldt, Zurich; Thomas Gibson, Thomas Gibson Fine Art Ltd; Desmond Corcoran, Lefevre Gallery; Dr Peter Nathan, Galerie Nathan, Zurich; Robert Schmit, Galerie Schmit, Paris; Michel Strauss, Sotheby's; John Tancock, Sotheby's, New York. Private collectors have responded to *The Private Degas* with great sympathy, and I am most grateful to those who have lent to the exhibition. I would also like to express my thanks to Peter Burton, David Daniels, Clifford and Jill Drake, Huw and Amy McGill, Sara Pappworth, Michael Pollard, Professor Theodore Reff, Gaye Smith and, *bien entendu*, my wife Belinda. My sanity has been saved by the administrative efforts of Judith Kimmelman and Julia Willcock, while Michael Harrison has given patient and thoughtful support throughout. It has been my privilege to have 'shared' Degas with the scholars whose exhibitions and publications have deepened our knowledge of his work over the last few years. Discussing Degas with Richard Kendall and George Shackelford is always a delightful stimulus; my deepest thanks, as Pellegrini put it, *à vous*.

Richard Thomson.
Heaton Moor, October 1986.

# Introduction

Degas's achievements as an artist were colossal. His career spanned more than half a century, from the mid-1850s almost to the First World War, and his output was phenomenal; he left some 1500 paintings and pastels and several thousand drawings, to say nothing of his activities as sculptor and printmaker. Over the last two decades intensive research has thrown much new light on Degas, establishing a clear picture of the vast range of copies he made as a young artist, exhaustively annotating his notebooks, analysing in great detail his output of prints and monotypes, producing full accounts of the development of certain key works, and accumulating biographical information. Yet there is still much to be done. Degas's career is often framed within three almost mutually exclusive divisions: the now well-researched period as copyist and history painter from the mid-1850s to the mid-1860s, the celebrated and heavily scrutinized two decades in Naturalist and Impressionist circles, and the neglected and misunderstood late work from about 1890 onwards. Such a framework is artificial, and this fragmentation has ironically been encouraged by the best work on Degas, much of which has been on detailed aspects of his work.

*The Private Degas*, as both book and exhibition, is intended to provide a more panoramic view of this great career than is usual. Its aim is to explore the complexity of Degas's working methods, taking sometimes oblique and unfamiliar angles in the belief that the time is now ripe for a more unified account of his work, based on new research, close observation of the pictures and informed speculation. *The Private Degas* seeks out fresh patterns of continuity and discontinuity within the whole length of his career. Its emphasis is on Degas's studio practice, on how he built up his pictures, how he planned and altered them, how his imagination worked. It is concerned as much with how he conceived his images as how he executed them. Many of Degas's ambitions, creative practices and notions about the purposes of art were formed during his early years, and the rest of his career was a rich dialogue with these. *The Private Degas* is centred on selected themes that are intended to demonstrate these undercurrents in Degas's art. The most important theme is the effect of his intensive period of copying on his later work and the different removes at which these influences were felt, for at times Degas's allusion to past art was overt and deliberate, at others implicit or unconscious. Others are the interrelationship of media, especially sculpture, in the genesis of his compositions, and the recurrence of certain poses and compositional formulae over lengthy periods of time. All these issues remain hitherto largely unexplored, especially in the format of an exhibition.

*The Private Degas* exhibits most of the subjects and media Degas employed over his long career, in appropriate proportions. With its stress on Degas's conceptions of picture-making, on private studio decisions, it deals less with famous finished works (the province of a major retrospective to be held in 1988) than with work-in-progress – the drawing, the oil sketch, the experiment – that is often of great beauty in its own right. 'Private' is not understood here as 'clandestine' or 'intimate', but rather in terms of the intellectual and practical problems of producing images that were raised and solved behind closed studio doors. Thus the brothel monotypes, which I take to be 'private', even fantasy images, are scarcely represented, while Degas's constant questioning of the means and function of drawing is an important subtext to my arguments. *The Private Degas*'s structure is loosely chronological, with both grouped and recurrent themes. The text can be read either as a continuous essay or as observations about a particular issue or group of works; it is dominated by the selection and thematic structure of the exhibition. Limitations of space have not always allowed discussion of other authors' views, and I fully acknowledge my debts to Degas scholarship, notably that of Ronald Pickvance, George Shackelford, and, above all, Theodore Reff.

# The result of reflection
# and study of the great masters

Throughout his career, Degas made it clear that he thought about his art in terms of the great masters whom he had studied as a young man. In 1874, at the age of forty, while he was preparing for the first Impressionist exhibition and completing one of his finest ballet paintings (66), he explained to the writer Edmond de Goncourt his ambition to parallel qualities he found in Mantegna and Veronese.[1] Fifteen years later George Moore, the Irish art critic, quoted publicly Degas's now famous disclaimer: 'no art was ever less spontaneous than mine. What I do is the result of reflection and study of the great masters; of inspiration, spontaneity, temperament . . . I know nothing'.[2] Degas was fond of paradox, of course, but he was not just trying with false modesty to denigrate his proven abilities to represent the modern world in flux, to produce peerless im-

ages of mobility, atmosphere and instantaneity; rather, he was attempting to explain how he worked, and to root his private studio practice in his deep knowledge of the old masters.

Degas's fascination with past art falls into three phases. From the time he left school and decided to become an artist, in 1853, and through a lengthy gestation to early maturity in the later 1860s, he copied prolifically, travelling France and Italy to visit museums and print-rooms. For some two decades, from the late 1860s, his active interest in old master art lay almost fallow. Nevertheless, if he made only rare copies during that time, the lessons he had learnt as a young man had a discreet influence on the naturalistic images of modern Paris with which he made such a reputation at the Impressionist exhibitions. From the later 1880s, Degas's enthusiasm for the art

of the past took on a new dimension. This change came about, in large part, through developments – one might even say crises – in his own art, and it manifested itself not only in a renewed spate of active copying, but also in the growth of Degas's own collection, which, if it emphasized the work of his contemporaries, also included paintings by El Greco, Perronneau and even Cuyp, as well as magisterial groups of work by Ingres and Delacroix.[3] Degas believed that any serious artist should have a deep and sympathetic understanding of earlier art, and would reap its full benefits through copying. As he told the dealer Ambroise Vollard late in life: 'One must copy and recopy the masters, and it is only having given every proof of being a good copyist that permission could reasonably be given to paint a radish from life.'[4]

'Make copies, young man, many copies.
You can only become a good artist by copying the masters.'
Ingres to Degas, 1855.[5]

Degas came from a well-to-do banking family, which had intermarried with the Italian aristocracy, and no serious objection seems to have been made to his artistic vocation. Inevitably he was steered along the conventional paths of art education. He was given initial tuition by

Félix Barrias, who had won the prestigious Prix de Rome in 1844, and later Louis Lamothe, a pupil of Ingres. Degas registered to copy at the Louvre on 7 April 1853, and two days later at the print room of the Bibliothèque Impériale (now the Bibliothèque Nationale).[6] His

tuition would have been conservative, and he would have been encouraged to copy Antique sculpture, High Renaissance artists such as Raphael, and Poussin and Ingres, the mainstream of academic classicism upheld by the French art establishment.[7] Degas largely adhered to the expected canon in his earliest copies, which were often made after engravings.[8] Thus his very early and hesitant sheet of two figures from Raphael's *School of Athens* was not made from the fresco in Rome but in a print-room after an engraving in Ottley's *Italian School of Design* (73, 74). In due course he would have passed on to copying from paintings, and the slightly later sheet, still characterized by a student's deliberate and tame hatching, after one of the thieves in Mantegna's *Calvary* from the Louvre (1, 2); begins to show an independence in Degas's willingness to look at artists not quite within the recommended hierarchy.

Enrolled at the Ecole des Beaux-Arts in April 1855, Degas did not remain long. We do not know why, but the evidence does not suggest deep dissatisfaction with either teaching or curriculum. In fact in a notebook of 1856 he made a thumbnail compositional sketch of *The Return of Tobit*,[9] the Prix de Rome subject that year, an indication of a commitment to the Ecole's tuition system, which culminated in the prestigious Prix. However, he did not enter the competition, but left for Rome in July 1856, and spent most of the next three years in Italy.[10] His decision to abandon the Ecole after little more than a year may have been due to an instinct that independent study would advance his skills further than tuition, that copying the masters of the Renaissance firsthand would serve him better than being coached to paint history compositions to set formulae. The fact that he drew from the model at the French School in Rome, the Villa Medici, again suggests no deep-seated animosity towards the academic establishment. Indeed, he befriended Prix de Rome winners – Elie

Delaunay and Jean-Jacques Henner – and other students visiting Italy, such as Léon Bonnat and Gustave Moreau.

Traditional training involved the experience of many months in Italy copying the Antique and the Renaissance, as well as producing a number of one's own history paintings under their influence; the aim was to provide the young artist with a reservoir of idealized forms and established compositional formulae which he would be able to tap in his later career. These young men in the 1850s would have expected to devote their lives to *la grande peinture*, to subjects taken from the Bible, classical literature and edifying moments of history intended for moral purpose and public display in major institutional buildings such as churches and town halls. For Prix de Rome winners, this training was supervised. So when in 1861 Henner wished to paint Correggio's *Danaë* as his prescribed copy, officialdom stepped in, and he copied the standard Raphael.[11] But for artists independently in Italy there were no such constraints. Moreau and Degas, by virtue of their private means, were able to develop less conventional taste in their copies. They spent from December 1858 to March 1859 together in Florence[12] and, perhaps on the initiative of the older Moreau, began to study artists outside the set canons. In a number of cases their choices coincided; both copied Quattrocento as well as High Renaissance works – Botticelli's *Birth of Venus* and Benozzo Gozzoli's *Journey of the Magi* (3, 123), for instance – and Baroque equestrian portraits, Velasquez's *Philip IV* and Van Dyck's *Charles V*.[13] By this time Degas's copying had begun gradually to change its rationale; no longer did he simply copy to learn, to imitate how an accredited master had

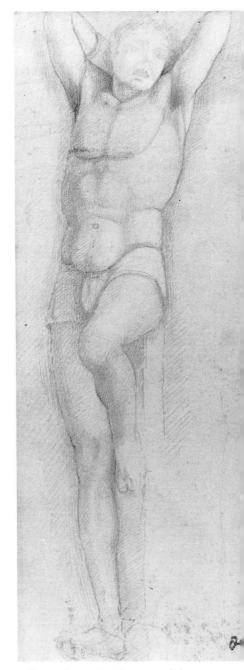

1 Degas, Copy after Mantegna, *Calvary: Crucified Thief*, c.1853–4. Pencil, heightened with red chalk. 31 × 13.5 cms. Zurich, Marianne Feilchenfeldt. CAT. 3

2 Mantegna, *Calvary*, *c.* 1457–9. Oil on panel. 67 × 93 cms. Paris, Musée du Louvre.

developed a form or composition, but rather to analyse an earlier image in order to gain specific information for his own paintings. His and Moreau's shared interest in horse subjects over that winter was in all probability the deliberate research for equestrian pictures on which they were about to embark. And in Degas's copy of Botticelli's *Venus* (3, 4) it is clear how his rather

gauche hatchings of previous years had softened and matured into a subtle painterly vehicle for transcribing the delicate modelling of the goddess's body. This greater sensitivity to light which Degas had recently developed via his copying is even more evident in his drawing after Michelangelo's *Dying Slave*, executed in Paris in 1859–60 (5, 6).[14]

This initial period of intense study of

old master art lasted well into the 1860s, with Degas in his mid-thirties and by now no longer painting history but modern life subjects and mixing with a new circle of artists and writers – Edouard Manet and James Tissot, Emile Zola and Edmond Duranty – concerned to tackle the contemporary world in their work. Degas registered as a copyist at the Louvre for the last time in March

11

3  Degas, Copy after Botticelli, *The Birth of Venus*, 1859. Pencil. 29 × 21 cms. Zurich, Marianne Feilchenfeldt. CAT. 11

12

4 Botticelli, *The Birth of Venus*, *c.*1485. Oil on canvas. 175 × 278.5 cms. Florence, Uffizi.

1868,[15] executing copies after Le Sueur's *St Paul preaching at Ephesus* and Mantegna's *Calvary* (99, 64). The *Calvary* is an intriguing apogee to this period of his career. On the one hand it shows a consistency in his studies and taste, for he had copied from this Mantegna some fifteen years before. On the other, it indicates the confidence with which this practice had filled him, for the full-sized painted copy appears to have been executed directly with the brush with no underdrawing, a free and lively version of the original. And with hindsight one can see, even from this small cross-section

of Degas's 500-odd copies, how the copying procedure trained his eye and fuelled his imagination, for inherent in them are issues that would concern him deeply in later years: the unified contour around the nude, the frieze-like design and low relief, symmetry of pose, and the figure cut off by the picture edge.

It was the purpose of copying to provide such initiatives, of course. As his father wrote to Degas in Florence late in 1858: 'One must detect and capture the artifices of the great masters, but shrug off all restraint in front of nature and represent it solely by one's own

inspiration.'[16] In later life Degas was fond of repeating this conventional wisdom. The secret, he would say, 'is to follow the advice the masters give you in their works while doing something different from them.'[17] Above all, he greatly valued working from memory, one's recollection tempered by the lessons of the past: 'paintings made in that way by a man with a cultivated memory, who knows his *métier* and the masters well, are almost always remarkable works; think of Delacroix!'[18] It is important to remember that in the nineteenth century studying the old masters as a mature

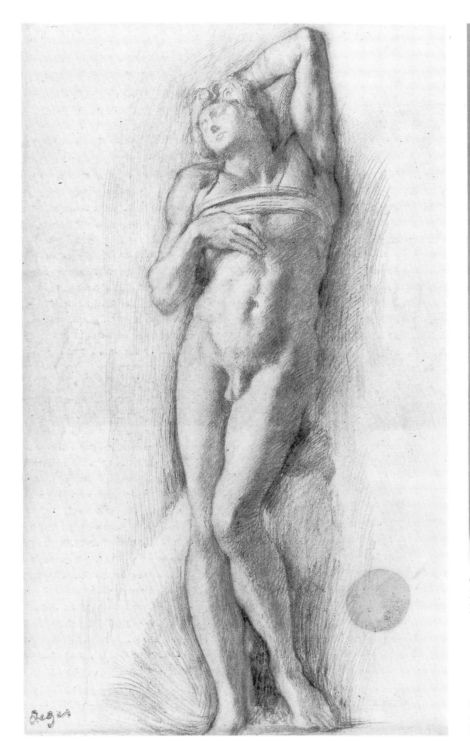

**6** Michelangelo, *Dying Slave*, 1513–16. Marble. Height: 215 cms. Paris, Musée du Louvre.

**5** Degas, Copy after Michelangelo, *Dying Slave*, *c.*1859–60. Pencil. 33 × 23 cms. Zurich, Marianne Feilchenfeldt. CAT. 14

artist was not considered demeaning or unimaginative but necessarily challenging and restorative. Ingres's last work, at 87, was a copy after Giotto; Delacroix travelled to Belgium in 1839 expressly to study Rubens. For artists of Degas's generation the experience of this copying and studying was an ever-present influence. This might well be literally so; both Henner and Degas kept copies they had made on view in their studios.[19] It also instilled a way of seeing, of observing the world and one's own work through the prism of old master art. Thus, to continue the comparison, Henner would write in a Roman notebook of 1860: 'The rooves . . . are in a very distinct pale red, a bit like the colour of women's hair in Titian and Veronese',[20] while Degas, making colour notes for a history painting at about the same time, suggested to himself contrasts 'rather like the values of Veronese's heads' in a picture in the Louvre.[21] And if Henner's Roman notebooks are full of variations on Titian's *Sacred and Profane Love* (Rome, Borghese Gallery) which prefigure many of his later groups of nudes,[22] if his *Bara* of the Salon of 1882 (Paris, Petit Palais) is based on a sketch made in the Louvre after Prud'hon's *Justice and Vengeance pursuing Crime*, might one not expect some similarly consistent response to past art on the part of Degas?

'Portraiture will be the most beautiful jewel in your crown.'
Auguste de Gas, 1858.[23]

Portraiture accounts for about one-fifth of Degas's huge production, and spans his whole career from the mid-1850s to the early twentieth century, although portraits begin to fall off in numbers after about 1890.[24] To gauge Degas's development from a young artist dependent on established prototypes through an emergent naturalism that challenged the contemporary stereotypes of portraiture to the assured maturity of the great portraits of the late 1870s, we are focusing here on two specific aspects of his portraiture: his rather formal – profile or frontal – heads and busts of women, and his more casually posed, full-length or seated, images of men, particularly of artistic colleagues.

Most of Degas's early portraits were of his immediate family, convenient sitters. His life-size head of his sister Thérèse in profile (7), drawn in sharp pencil of even pressure with a conscientious diagonal hatching in careful emulation of Raphaelesque portrait drawings, must date from about 1855–6, prior to Degas's Italian sojourn. He also drew her half-turned towards the spectator, again life-size, on pink paper of identical dimensions;[25] already he was aware of the value of seeing a form from several directions. While in Italy he copied portraits in both paintings and drawings, chiefly after acknowledged masters of the genre such as Titian, Pontormo, Van Dyck and Velasquez. One of the most intriguing of these is a sheet of studies now in Cleveland (65). Degas must have added the inscription 'Flor. 1857' in later life, for he was not in Florence that year. He was, however, in 1858, the year that

Moreau copied the silverpoint head of a young woman, then attributed to Leonardo, which is at the centre of Degas's sheet (8).[26] Degas scrupulously rendered the head in a hatching which echoed the silverpoint of the original, more subtle than in his earlier portrait of his sister. But with scant concern for his delicate copy, he used the margins of the sheet for other drawings, in pen, ink and coloured wash, which indicate the variety of his interests at this time. A notebook used in Florence in 1858–9 includes a number of copies after the Uffizi Leonardos which are consistent with the silverpoint head,[27] and also many studies made in preparation for Degas's large portrait *The Bellelli Family* (1858–60; Paris, Musée d'Orsay).[28] It may be that the bonneted head of a girl to the upper right of the Cleveland drawing is one of Degas's Bellelli cousins. Again, the female nude drawn horizontally tallies with nothing in Degas's own *oeuvre* but is remarkably similar to figures by contemporaries who were in Florence at that time. The nude is close to one in Moreau's *Daughters of Thespius* (Paris, Musée Gustave Moreau), a huge canvas started in 1853, and also to Delaunay's *Diana* (Paris, Musée d'Orsay) which, although exhibited at the Salon of 1872, was based on drawings made in Italy in the 1850s.[29] Did Degas have access to his friends' drawings, or were they all working from a common source? Whatever the answer, the Cleveland sheet of studies is indicative of Degas's determination to improve his abilities as a portrait draughtsman by copying Renaissance masters, his shared interests

7 Degas, *Thérèse de Gas*, c.1855–6. Pencil. 28.5 × 23.6 cms. Cambridge, Fitzwilliam Museum. CAT. 8

8 Circle of Leonardo da Vinci, *Head of a Woman*. Silverpoint. 59.6 × 39.3 cms. Florence, Uffizi.

with his academic colleagues, and his voracious use of drawing, so evident in his notebooks but crystallized in this one sheet, to emulate, observe and invent.

As he began his independent career in Paris during the early 1860s Degas seems to have begun to question the accepted conventions of portraiture, based on standardized assumptions about gender and its representation. In Ingres's portraits, for example, men are shown as forceful presences, often out-of-doors, whereas women are regularly depicted sitting indoors, stressing their cultivated grace and materialistic status – appropriate for aristocratic or *grande bourgeoise* sitters – rather than individual character. In Degas's double-portrait of his sister Thérèse and her husband Edmondo Morbilli, probably executed shortly after their wedding in 1863, one can detect tension between convention and innovation (9). Its preparation was traditional. Degas made at least four preliminary drawings – one for each figure and two drapery studies for Thérèse's crinoline[30] – and studied his sister's head in an exquisite monochrome oil sketch, alert to her calm dignity (11). The composition adhered to the conventional roles exemplified in, say, Ingres's portrait drawings, with the male posed casually and placed in a proprietorial position, with the woman passively seated (10). However, Degas was not entirely happy with this, and seems to have given his sister more purpose by representing her embroidering. In later years he took up the portrait again, scraping down and reworking both Thérèse's finely rendered crinoline and her more innovative activity, perhaps trying to give the canvas yet more the quality of a genre painting by adding the figure who disappears through the door to the right.

Degas achieved greater naturalistic immediacy with his portrait of the painter Victoria Dubourg, executed about 1866 (12). By now a friend of Edmond Duranty, an art critic and expert on physiognomy, Degas was starting to explore theories of gesture and expression to enhance the psychological accuracy

and immediate modernity in his work. Notebooks of this period include notes on Lavater's physiognomic theories of earlier in the century, which Degas evidently sought to refine,[31] and it is no coincidence that in one of these is Degas's initial idea for the Dubourg portrait.[32] He instructed himself: 'Do portraits of people in their familiar, typical postures, above all give their face the same range of expressions as one gives their body. So if the smile is typical of the person, make them smile.'[33] His preparatory drawing of her head and shoulders (13) shows how he had developed his rather idealized handling of the previous decade, the hatching softly registering the fall of light as he investigates the idiosyncracies of the sitter: the not-quite-direct angle of the head, the gently penetrating gaze, full nostrils and slight smile. In another sheet he recorded the exact way in which she clasped her hands.[34] The final painting is a remarkable image, showing the young woman seated forward in her chair, a posture bespeaking candour and confidence, found more conventionally in male portraits. It is possible that Degas's copy after Antonio Moro's *Elisabeth de Valois* (14) also dates from the later 1860s, though it is uncertain when he would have had access to the original.[35] Degas did not use stump to bring out highlights after the 1860s, and the head seen from a slight angle and lit from the left has parallels in his female portraits of that period, such as *Victoria Dubourg* and *Mlle Gaujelin* (1867; Boston, Isabella Stuart Gardner Museum). This powerful copy would have had no immediate relevance to these paintings, but would have helped Degas see how a predecessor had coped with a pictorial issue of general consequence to his current portraits.

9 Degas, *Edmondo and Thérèse Morbilli*,
*c*.1863–4. Oil on canvas. 117.1 × 89.9 cms.
Washington, National Gallery of Art.

10 Ingres, *Lord and Lady William Cavendish
Bentinck*, 1816. Pencil. 30.1 × 22.2 cms.
Bayonne, Musée Bonnat.

11 Degas, Study for *Edmondo and Thérèse
Morbilli*, *c*.1863–4. Oil on canvas.
37 × 29 cms. Zurich, private collection.
CAT. 23

**12** Degas, *Victoria Dubourg*, *c*. 1866. Oil on canvas. 81 × 65 cms. Toledo Museum of Art.

**13** Degas, Study for *Victoria Dubourg*, *c*. 1866. Pencil and black chalk. 31.1 × 22.2 cms. The Cleveland Museum of Art. CAT. 30

**14** Degas, Copy after Moro, *Elisabeth of Valois*, *c*. 1865–70. Black chalk, charcoal, and stump. 40.5 × 27.4 cms. Cambridge, Fitzwilliam Museum. CAT. 29

15 Degas, *Portrait of a Woman*, c.1876–8. Monotype. 21.5 × 16 cms. The Art Institute of Chicago. CAT. 52

*en-page* of *Portrait of a Woman* shows Degas's mastery of the medium, toning down the background, thinning the ink with turpentine, smudging the features most delicately to evoke the melancholy mien of the sitter. She has been speculatively identified as the actress Ellen André.[37] Popular illustration of the period customarily codified the diverse population of Paris into types, giving enough pictorial information to convey class and occupation (16). Degas's monotype is as much a proletarian type as a portrait. His crowded ballet and racecourse scenes of the 1870s were founded on such codification, and this monotype demonstrates how, in reaction to his early training, the naturalist aesthetic predominant in his mid-career required him to rehearse the pictorial syntax of the illustrated press.

16 Champollion, *The Grisette*, 1876. Etching. 6.5 × 5 cms. From: *Paris à l'Eau-Forte*, 7 November 1876, opp. p.60. Paris, Bibliothèque Nationale.

Degas's consummate skill as a portraitist is evident from his monotype *Portrait of a Woman* (15). He began to experiment with this novel medium in the mid-1870s.[36] Monotype is a hybrid, a printed drawing. A metal plate is either covered with ink which is then partially removed to produce an image (the dark-field manner) or the image is made in ink on a blank plate (the light-field manner), and in each case is then put through a press. Only one 'true' proof can be made; subsequent impressions are increasingly faint, and Degas would use them as the ground for pastels. The technical confidence and suave *mise-*

From the 1880s onwards Degas rarely made portraits except in pastel. Just as he had adjusted his medium and handling in his student days to the requirements of the project in hand, so he did in middle age. For a drawing such as the *Portrait of a Seated Woman* (17), executed about 1885, was first given a structure in charcoal, a broad, friable medium that allowed for bold forms and contours necessary to Degas's weak eyesight, and then worked in pastel, allowing him to colour and mould his motif without surrendering an active linearity. We do not know the name of the sitter, though the patch on her left shoulder identifies her as a violinist, rather than a dancer as has previously been thought.[38] Degas contrived to use urgent, even rough, means to give a sensitive account of her personality, placing her in an agitated pose, charting her stubborn jaw and heavy eyelids, accenting her anaemic complexion with lavender and green. Here indeed is the culmination of his schemes of the late 1860s, for the body provides as many clues as the face about the woman's tense character.

It is not known when Degas began to sculpt portraits, but he certainly completed a large bust of Hortense Valpinçon in 1884 which soon fell apart due to his poor workmanship.[39] Almost a decade later, in 1893, he made a head of the ballet dancer Mlle Salle (18) alongside his friend the sculptor Bartholomé, who

18 Degas, Study for the *Portrait of Mlle Salle*, 1893. Bronze. Height: 27 cms. Fridart Foundation. CAT. 88

17 Degas, *Portrait of a Seated Woman*, *c*.1885. Pastel and charcoal. 63.8 × 49.5 cms. Manchester, Whitworth Art Gallery. CAT. 80

was producing a more ambitious seated portrait of her;[40] gossip had it that Salle was Bartholomé's mistress.[41] In 1886 Degas had made a pastel showing her head in three positions[42] – much as Van Dyck had of Charles I (Royal Collection) and Philippe de Champaigne of Richelieu (London, National Gallery) for Bernini – and it may well be that Degas was planning a sculpture of Salle at that time, but held off until 1893. The head is broad and approximate, and the caesura between scalp and forehead suggests that it was never fully resolved. Yet there is evidence of careful working, with a comb used to give texture to hair and face, and the application of small particles of matter suggesting painstaking work. Degas, as in *Victoria Dubourg* or the monotype we have discussed, displayed a vivid awareness of facial asymmetry, in his modelling of Salle's nose for instance, and also of the fall of light, for the unconventionally treated left eye may well be intended to approximate to the less 'finished' state of a form in shadow.

LEFT
**19** Anon., *Auguste de Gas*, c.1855. Daguerreotype. Dimensions and location unknown.

ABOVE
**20** Degas, *Portrait of Gustave Moreau*, c.1860. Oil on canvas. 40 × 22 cms. Paris, Musée Gustave Moreau. CAT. 15

By contrast, the male portrait did not require Degas gradually to break down such inhibiting conventions of representation as the female. While he could work in a formal, authoritative vein when appropriate – as in *Achille de Gas in the Uniform of a Naval Cadet* (*c*.1855; Washington, National Gallery of Art) – he favoured the casual and relaxed. Indeed, the image of a man seated in an informal fashion was itself a stock formula in early photography, as Degas was no doubt well aware, on the evidence of a photograph of his father (19) and another pasted into a notebook in the early 1860s.[43] Such slovenly body language was almost unthinkable in female portraiture at this period, but Degas was swift to use it in his representations of men. His portrait of Moreau (20), executed about 1860 shortly after their return from Italy, differs greatly from the traditional, patrician motif of Degas that Moreau had planned.[44] Degas gave no indication of setting, but the presence of the sitter's discarded hat and gloves marks him as a well-groomed bourgeois visitor, caught quickly on a call to Degas's studio. The sense of immediacy is enhanced by Moreau's energetic, even argumentative gaze and gesture, as well as by the rapid execution. Three etchings of Edouard Manet follow the prototype of *Gustave Moreau*.[45] In the most developed of these Manet sits sideways in his chair, hands clasped and legs drawn in, with an air of introspection (21). A top-hat lies on the floor, and behind him stretched canvases lean face to the

**21** Degas, *Manet Seated, turned to the right*, *c*.1864–5. Etching and drypoint.
19.5 × 13 cms. The Art Institute of Chicago.
CAT. 24

22 Degas, Study for *James Tissot*, c.1866–8. Black chalk and pencil. 31 × 35 cms. Cambridge, Mass., Fogg Art Museum. CAT. 31

wall. There is a distinct ambiguity about whether Manet is a visitor or seated in his own studio. Degas appears satisfied to have left this compact, meditative image as a print, but he developed the idea in a painted portrait of another colleague. He began to explore James Tissot with two studies of the head[46] and then a drawing of the whole conception (22). Tissot is seated in an urbane, assertive fashion, left hand on hip and legs stretched out wide, directing his gaze at the spectator. Sensing that this was not quite apt for the nervy, careerist Tissot, Degas revised the pose in a thumbnail sketch in a notebook,[47] draping the left arm limply over the chair and retracting the legs to the more self-contained position he had used for Manet. Refined further in two other drawings,[48] this pose served for the large painted portrait (23). Degas was still making decisions on canvas. He changed the position of the cane, once laid across Tissot's lap, and specified the images in the background that add rather ambiguous information about the tastes of Tissot or the artist in whose studio he sits.[49] The portrait of Tissot is thus an intriguing instance of Degas's use of earlier images to fuel new projects, of his restless use of drawing, notebook, and canvas to recast the details of pose, gesture, physiognomy, costume and environment to provide a multi-faceted visualization of the sitter's personality.

Degas's portraiture took on new degrees of refinement and spontaneity in the 1870s, in parallel with the ideas propounded by Duranty in *La Nouvelle Peinture* of 1876, above all the link between posture and personality.[50] Duranty, a great admirer of Daumier, was well aware that the painter had much to learn in this respect from the caricaturist. So, despite his earlier admiration of portraits in the grand manner, was Degas. Among his friends in the 1870s was the Italian caricaturist Carlo Pellegrini, then working in London for the society magazine *Vanity Fair*.[51] His address appears in notebooks of the 1875-8 period,[52] and he probably drew his caricature of Degas on a visit to England at that time (24).[53] Degas's own *portrait-charge* of Pellegrini seems to be a retort to it, to judge by its witty signature (25). Using a full-length format typical of Pellegrini's own caricatures (26),[54] it views him from above, flattering his stout figure and catching him in characteristically animated pose. Ingres had advised that the initial drawing for a portrait should be 'a sort of caricature',[55] and it was in this way that Degas began his portrait of the art critic Diego Martelli, another Italian friend, who spent the winter of 1878-9 in Paris. His first drawing, which has been removed from a notebook,[56] is a hastily executed sketch of the dumpy Martelli seated at a desk, his facial features recorded with exaggeration (27). It formed the basis for a horizontal composition (28), prior to which Degas had refined Martelli's portrait in two highly finished drawings.[57] Dissatisfied with this format, Degas made another rapid notebook

23 Degas, *James Tissot*, c.1866-8. Oil on canvas. 151.4 × 112.1 cms. New York, The Metropolitan Museum of Art, Purchase, Rogers Fund, 1939.

27

24 Pellegrini, *Degas*, *c.* 1876–7. Medium, measurements and location unknown. From Lafond, I, p. 107.

LEFT
25 Degas, *Carlo Pellegrini*, *c.* 1876–7. *Essence*, watercolour and pastel. 63.2 × 34 cms. London, Tate Gallery.
CAT. 51

26 Pellegrini, *Conservative Conversion* (Lord Wharncliffe). Lithograph, from *Vanity Fair*, 14 August 1875. London, National Portrait Gallery.

27 Degas, Study for *Diego Martelli*, 1879.
Pencil. 11.1 × 16.7 cms. Edinburgh,
National Gallery of Scotland. CAT. 60

28 Degas, *Diego Martelli*, 1879. Oil on
canvas. 75 × 110 cms. Buenos Aires, Museo
Nacional de Bellas Artes.

sketch[58] and two further drawings which extended the figure full-length (29).[59] From these he executed the final version of the portrait, which he exhibited at the 1879 Impressionist exhibition (30). The Martelli portrait has an extraordinary vitality, the squat, gregarious Italian caught in a pensive moment and habitual pose. Clearly Degas had this end in mind from his earliest notebook sketch, but the subtle spontaneity of the exhibited canvas had to be developed through a twice-repeated cycle of sketches, preparatory drawings and oil painting.

Degas's double portrait of Paul Lafond and Alphonse Cherfils (71) must date from about the same time as the Martelli portrait, to judge by comparison with Carolus-Duran's 1871 painting of Cherfils, which shows the same handsome nose set in a less full face (31). Degas's is a truly private portrait, for not only does it show two close friends, one a museum curator, the other a collector, engaged in the mutually agreeable study of a canvas, but it was also dedicated to them. Painted on panel – possibly the lid of a large cigar-box – in monochrome, it was evidently executed at speed, perhaps in one sitting on a visit to their Pyrenean home-town, Pau. Nevertheless, Degas has masterfully contrasted their physiques and physiognomies. A panel, rather than a canvas,

**29** Degas, Study for *Diego Martelli*, 1879. Black chalk, heightened with white. 45 × 29 cms. England, private collection. CAT 61

OPPOSITE
**30** Degas, *Diego Martelli*, 1879. Oil on canvas. 110 × 100 cms. Edinburgh, National Gallery of Scotland.

**31** Carolus-Duran, *Alphonse Cherfils*, 1871.
Oil on canvas. 58 × 43 cms. Pau, Musée des
Beaux-Arts.

**32** Degas, *The Dancing Master Jules Perrot*,
*c*.1880. Oil on panel. 35.5 × 26 cms.
Formerly Mrs Frances Tarson.

**33** Degas, *The Dancing Master Jules Perrot*,
*c*.1880. Black and brown chalk.
49.5 × 33.2 cms. Mr David Daniels. CAT. 65

physiognomy and environment into a total likeness. But Degas's awareness of past portraiture did not leave him. In the 1890s he posed himself and his housekeeper Zoé Closier for a photograph (34). His arrangement slyly echoes that of Ingres's *The Composer Luigi Cherubini* (35), a portrait he had copied as a student,[60] in which the pensive artist likewise sits brooding, but attended by a muse rather than a *bonne!* With Degas, reverence was often mixed with irony.

was also used at this time for a portrait of the great dancer and choreographer Jules Perrot (32). The painting was made from a superb drawing of the proud old man, no doubt done from life (33). With a sure hatching and fluency of line shared with the Martelli drawings, Degas achieved a startling sense of the bulk and stiffness now frustrating this once so agile body. Perrot reached seventy in 1880, and his seated portrait may have been made to mark this anniversary.

Degas's portraiture should be seen as a transformation from convention to naturalism. Only gradually did his female portraits move from old master prototypes and contemporary bourgeois requirements of grace and dignity towards a more informal, indeed physical, representation of women, a possibility always available for male portraits. In these, and particularly his images of artistic colleagues, he manipulated pose,

34 Degas, *Degas and Zoé Closier, c.*1890–5. Photograph. Paris, Bibliothèque Nationale. CAT. 82

35 Ingres, *The Composer Luigi Cherubini*, 1842. Oil on canvas. 105 × 94 cms. Paris, Musée du Louvre.

## The Young Spartans Exercising: 'That doesn't count.'
### Degas to Rouault.[61]

Degas's *The Young Spartans Exercising* was not his first history painting but it was perhaps the one that was of greatest significance for his later career. It seems to have been begun about 1860, with a major bout of work over a couple of years, then taken up again around 1865, and perhaps once more in the later 1870s. The project, which involved a number of notebook sketches, some sixteen drawings, four oil sketches and two substantial canvases, centred on three pivotal versions of the design. The canvas featuring trees and a temple, now in Chicago (36), seems to have been realized quite rapidly. Then Degas revised the design in an oil sketch (72), which he transferred to the large London canvas (37), substantial portions of which he later overpainted.[62] He deployed the stable compositional conventions of academic Neo-Classicism throughout, based on two groups of facing figures arranged in a frieze-like format on the first plane, with a subsidiary central focus to enhance the illusion of depth. This formula was

33

**36** Degas, *The Young Spartans Exercising*, *c*.1860. Oil on canvas. 97.4 × 140 cms. The Art Institute of Chicago.

**37** Degas, *The Young Spartans*, *c*.1860–1 (reworked later). Oil on canvas. 109.2 × 154.3 cms. London, National Gallery.

absolutely standard. Ingres was only one of many Prix de Rome winners to have used it, in his *Achilles receiving the Ambassadors of Agamemnon* (38). Even Degas's solution to break the monotony of the frieze by introducing a crouching figure was a convention,[63] and his kneeling youth is close to the one who fills a corner in Baudry's prize-winning *Zenobia discovered on the Banks of the Araxes* (1850; Paris, Ecole des Beaux-Arts). Individual elements of *The Young Spartans* were also derived from academically respectable sources. While several of the background figures were borrowed from Antique sculpture[64] the dramatic pose of the youth with raised arms is a variant on Ingres's stained-glass cartoon of the *Archangel Raphael* (39), which Degas had copied at the Universal Exhibition of 1855.[65]

But for all these efforts to produce a history painting according to orthodox prescriptions, *The Young Spartans* reveals a restless dissatisfaction that became increasingly typical of Degas's creative practice. This is evident not only in his recastings of the design and his willingness to overpaint, but also in his concern to repeat and revise poses. The dynamic yet delicate sheet for the boy with the upraised arms now in Detroit (40) was made in preparation for the Chicago canvas. Certainly its hatching and the way Degas made rhythmic marks around the figure to give it a low relief are reminiscent of other drawings of about 1860, such as the copy after Michelangelo's *Dying Slave* (5). But he reworked the pose full-length in another sheet (41), prior to painting the small Fogg oil sketch, with an economy typical of the other drawings made at this intermediate stage (43). Yet even after this oil sketch more drawings were required to refine poses further. A fine life study

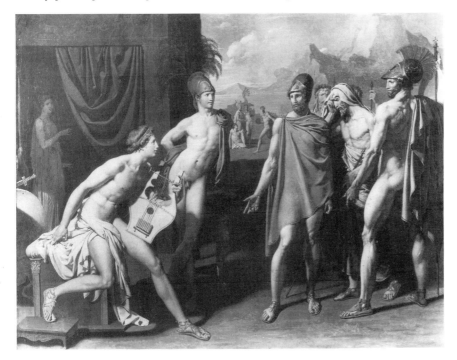

38 Ingres, *Achilles receiving the Ambassadors of Agamemnon*, 1801. Oil on canvas. 113 × 146 cms. Paris, École des Beaux-Arts.

**39** Ingres, *The Archangel Raphael*, 1842. Oil on canvas. 210 × 92 cms. Paris, Musée du Louvre.

**40** Degas, Study for *The Young Spartans*, *c*.1860. Pencil. 28.5 × 17.7 cms. Detroit Institute of Arts. CAT. 17

36

of a girl (42) was made for the London picture, her left hand moved up to clasp her impetuous colleague's arm, and posed almost in the reverse of the equally tentative boy on the opposing side of the picture (44). For all *The Young Spartans'* conventional structure, its actual execution – the evidence of Degas's private deliberations in the studio – indicates that a number of the elements usually considered typical of his later practice were evident by the early 1860s. The repeated drawing of the same pose to move from detail to simplicity, the working of variations on the same motif over an extended period, and the echoing of poses within the same design to give compositional coherence are all to be found in the dancer and bather subjects that dominated his work after 1890.

Despite the elderly Degas's disclaimer, *The Young Spartans* did count. Along with other history paintings and copies, he kept it visible in his studio late in life,[66] and it was included in the catalogue of the 1880 Impressionist exhibition, though it appears Degas did not in the end show this link between his artistic past and present.[67] Nor did *The Young Spartans* lose its place in his imagination. Its design is faintly mirrored in a drawing he made in the mid-1880s of five ballet dancers, whose co-ordinated movements culminate in the arched arms of a stretching figure, in front of a set featuring a classical ruin (45). In *The Young Spartans* Degas had aimed to honour the unashamed athleticism of

41 Degas, Study for *The Young Spartans: Youth with Arms Upraised*, *c*.1860–1. Pencil and black chalk. 31.7 × 19.4 cms. New York, The Metropolitan Museum of Art, Lehman Collection. CAT. 18

37

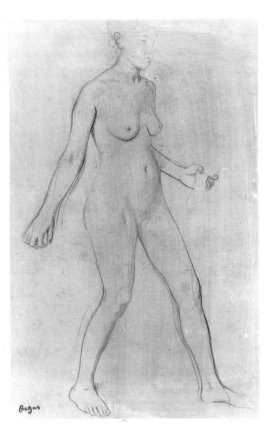

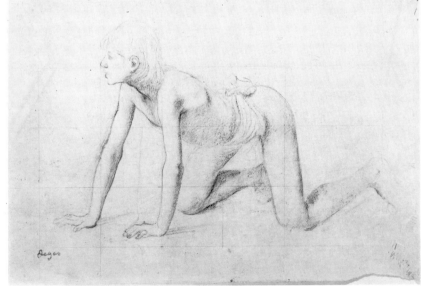

**42** Degas, Study for *The Young Spartans: Standing Girl*, *c.*1860–1. Pencil. 36.9 × 23.3 cms. Private collection. CAT. 20

**43** Degas, Study for *The Young Spartans: Youth in an attitude of defence*, *c.*1860–1. Pencil and black chalk. 43.3 × 21.3 cms. New York, Metropolitan Museum of Art, Lehman Collection. CAT. 19

**44** Degas, Study for *The Young Spartans: Kneeling Youth*, *c.*1860–1. Pencil and black chalk. 22.8 × 35.2 cms. Toledo Museum of Art. CAT. 21

the youth of Ancient Greece.[68] If his justification for painting the ballet was that 'it is all that is left to us of the combined movement of the Greeks',[69] how appropriate it is that a drawing of the dance should be reminiscent of *The Young Spartans* made a quarter of a century before.

**45** Degas, *Five Dancers, c.*1884–8. Black chalk. 38 × 53 cms. Location unknown. (Vente III, no. 180).

> 'Without actually imitating his manner, one can
> follow a good many paths along which he has lit real torches.'
> Delacroix on Veronese, 1859.[70]

It is usually considered that the second half of the 1860s witnessed a clean break for Degas, who moved abruptly away from history painting to contemporary subjects. But the transition, such as it was, was more gradual and complex, the lessons of past art still being digested. One of the most important paintings of this period was shown at the Salon of 1868 under the title *Portrait de Mlle E.F. . . . à propos de la ballet 'La Source'* (46). A portrait of the ballerina Eugénie Fiocre in a ballet which had opened in November 1866,[71] its significance lay not only in the fact that it was a large-scale, up-to-the-minute Salon picture, but also that by its very title it made play with the knowledge of artifice. Degas

stressed that it was a painted recreation of what was originally only a performance. His highly finished figures and scrupulous reflections echoed the use of real water and a live horse; thus artifice was piled upon artifice.

The actual genesis of *Mlle Fiocre* is uncertain, and X-ray examination of the Salon picture – once heavily varnished, poorly cleaned, and then retouched – would reveal much. It appears that the horse's head was not originally lowered towards the water, but in fact raised in profile to the left, behind Eugénie Fiocre. If this were so, the painting would have had a flat, frieze-like effect. A drawing in a notebook may have been an initial idea for revising the design, in particular

by making the horse drink;[72] it is still, however, a somewhat shallow arrangement (47). The alteration of the horse was probably introduced through the intermediary of sculpture. Degas's statuette *Horse Drinking* has a high finish similar to his equine drawings of the 1860s, one of which may have been used as a study for it (48, 49), and it must date from this period. It may not have been made specifically as a study for *Mlle Fiocre*; nevertheless, its pose tallies with the horse in the exhibited painting and its introduction served to emphasize Fiocre herself and to add a contradictory thrust to the now diagonal bank. Degas had settled the pose of Fiocre and a subsidiary maid in an oil sketch, and had drawn

**46** Degas, *Portrait of Mlle Eugénie Fiocre, à propos the ballet 'La Source'*, *c.*1866–8. Oil on canvas. 130 × 144 cms. New York, Brooklyn Museum.

**47** Degas, Study for *Mlle Fiocre*, *c.*1866–8. 11.3 × 36 cms. Nb. 20, pp. 20–1. Paris, Musée du Louvre, Département des Arts Graphiques.

OPPOSITE, ABOVE
**48** Degas, *Horse Drinking*, *c.*1865–8. Bronze. Height: 16 cms. Private collection. CAT. 27

OPPOSITE, BELOW
**49** Degas, *Study of a Horse*, *c.*1865–8. Pencil, 23.7 × 26.3 cms. Rotterdam, Boymans-van Beuningen Museum. CAT. 26

the dancer from life in a large sheet (50, 51). Here she is shown languorous and melancholy, Degas's cursive drawing concentrating on personal details such as her face, arms and feet, rather than her costume, which he studied later from a professional model.[73] Degas just made a drawing for the figure of the maid with the mandolin who stabilizes the upper left corner (52). The cropping of her skirt and instrument shows that he knew precisely where to place her in relation to the main figure, and this sturdy drawing was enough to give him a basis from which to paint. *Mlle Fiocre* was created out of contradictions. In terms of its execution it demonstrates both Degas's conservative practices – establishing a figure nude and then drawing it draped, for example, just as academic artists like Delaunay would do[74] – and also his willingness to improvise with work in progress, in this case bringing sculpture into an already complicated repertoire of preparatory procedures. And for all the modernity and artfulness of *Mlle Fiocre*, its celebration of a chic ballerina more notorious for her expensive and much pursued charms than her dancing, and its conceits on reality and artifice, it is still rooted in Degas's experience as a copyist. For the overall conception – the oriental setting in which a richly attired woman and her maid-servants rest on the banks of a river – is that of the traditional *Finding of Moses* subject. Indeed, in a small canvas usually dated to the late 1860s[75] Degas copied Veronese's version of the subject in the Lyons museum (53, 54), and the diagonal design, the interrelationship of the women, one in profile and the other full-face, and even the brocaded colour of the costumes suggest that the Veronese was in Degas's mind as he planned *Mlle Fiocre*.

41

**50** Degas, Study for *Mlle Fiocre*, *c.*1866–8.
Oil on canvas. 81 × 65 cms. Buffalo,
Albright-Knox Art Gallery.

**51** Degas, Study for *Mlle Fiocre: Eugénie
Fiocre*, *c.*1866–8. Pencil. 45.1 × 28 cms.
Mr David Daniels. CAT. 32

OPPOSITE, LEFT
**52** Degas, Study for *Mlle Fiocre: Young
Woman playing a Mandolin*, *c.*1866–8.
Pencil. 35.5 × 21.4 cms. The Art Institute
of Chicago. CAT. 33

OPPOSITE RIGHT, ABOVE
**53** Degas, Copy after Veronese, *The Finding
of Moses*, *c.*1865–8. Oil on canvas.
31.2 × 17.3 cms. Cambridge, Fitzwilliam
Museum. CAT. 28

OPPOSITE RIGHT, BELOW
**54** Veronese (studio), *The Finding of Moses*,
*c.*1570–5. Oil on canvas. 129.5 × 115 cms.
Lyons, Musée des Beaux-Arts.

Degas's continuing dialogue with past art also has a clandestine presence in *The Duet* (or *The Singing Rehearsal*) (55). An initial sketch for the canvas appears in a notebook used chiefly in the late 1860s, to when this picture should be dated.[76] Degas prepared it with two large and vivid drawings, executed with brio from life. The finest is for the right-hand woman (57), apparently posed by Degas's sister Marguerite,[77] in which he established her alarmed features and timorous gesture with assured yet sensitive alacrity. In the other sheet (56) he substituted the melodramatic trailing arm for the more credible clasping of her score. The sophistication of this scene of performers in rehearsal extended beyond the articulation of pose,

**55** Degas, *The Duet (The Singing Rehearsal)*, *c*.1868–70. Oil on canvas. 81 × 65 cms. Washington, Dumbarton Oaks Research Library and Collection. CAT. 38 (Reproduced in colour on p. 58)

**56** Degas, Study for *The Duet*, *c*.1868–70. Pencil. 48.3 × 31.5 cms. Paris, Musée du Louvre, Département des Arts Graphiques.

44

57 Degas, Study for *The Duet*, *c*. 1868–70. Pencil. 49 × 31.2 cms. Paris, Musée du Louvre, Département des Arts Graphiques. CAT. 39

**58** Veronese (studio), *The Annunciation*, *c*. 1560–70. Oil on canvas. 99.5 × 129 cms. Genoa, Palazzo Rosso.

expression and gesture. Thinking like a theatre director himself, he imagined his actresses on the 'stage' of his picture, and the drawing for the right-hand figure includes two marginal sketches of the scene from above, schemas of the diagonal interrelationships of both pictorial construction and the psychological narrative. So alert was he to the emotional import of open space that he reduced what had once been a *chaise-longue* in the foreground to a mere armchair in order to emphasize the exchange between the women. Their deliberately explicit gestures of greeting and caution emulate the conventional composition of Annunciation scenes,[78] a design Degas must surely have used consciously. In a letter to Moreau of 1859 he had praised the Veroneses in the Palazzo Rosso at Genoa, one of which is an *Annunciation* (58) whose somewhat overplayed gesturing set within a crisply architectural space may well have returned to Degas's imagination as he composed *The Duet*.[79]

> '*He makes war on drawing with the weapons of a draughtsman.*'
>
> Jules Claretie, 1874.[80]

The dance played a dominant role in Degas's production during the 1870s, and as early as 1874 he had won a reputation as a specialist in ballet subjects.[81] Degas's motives for this obsession, which he sustained well into the twentieth century, were multifarious. He would claim that his interest was in movement, and in drawing: 'The dancer is only a pretext for drawing.'[82] Apt as this justification is for the images of the last twenty years of his career, his initial stimuli in the 1870s involved other factors. The collapse of the family bank in mid-decade and his self-imposed obligation to pay off large debts may have induced him to produce pictures of this saleable subject. The ballet encapsulates a rich complex of tensions, setting the apparent ease of performance against the actual agony of effort, allowing for ostensibly naturalistic images of people submitting their bodies to a confected discipline, and, given the mores of the Opéra in Third Republic Paris, providing a piquant combination of art on stage and vice backstage.

Degas's fascination with the dance developed slowly and tentatively. He produced only a handful of dance pictures between *Mlle Fiocre* and the two he sold to Durand-Ruel in 1872, *The Rehearsal Room* (New York, Metropolitan Museum) and *The Dance Rehearsal Room at the rue Le Peletier Opéra House* (59).[83] These early pictures have in common a distinct caution about representing vigorous movement; for all their variety of pose, they show exercising or the rehearsal of steps, not actual dancing. Both *Rehearsal Room* paintings are small and highly finished, reminiscent of the work of successful contemporaries such as Meissonier and Alfred Stevens; the figures are ordered within a lucid architectural space, similar to *The Duet*, and carefully delineated. It thus comes as something of a shock to find that the drawings for *The Dance Rehearsal Room* are not precise work in pencil, but broad and approximate sheets in *essence* on coloured paper.[84] *Essence* is paint from which much of the oil has been removed; the pigment is then thinned with a medium like turpentine for easier application, quicker drying, and broad effects. The most extraordinary of these preparatory drawings is *Two Dancers* (60). In the other studies the figures were picked out in pencil prior to being overworked in *essence*, and a grey wash was used to give the dancer relief. But *Two Dancers* was executed directly with the brush, perhaps even from memory rather than the posed model. Degas evidently intended only two figures, and then superimposed on the right-hand dancer the contours of the head and shoulders of another girl who masks her in the finished painting. These *essence* drawings conceived the figures on a far larger scale than they appear on the canvas. In other words, for these paintings of the early 1870s Degas was using the conventional phase of preparatory drawing to see big, to produce generalized forms to which he would add detail in this process of painting. It was a time for improvisation and reassessment, not that he disallowed alteration on canvas; the placement of the ballet-master, for instance,

**59** Degas, *The Dance Rehearsal Room at the rue Le Peletier Opéra House, c.*1871–2.
Oil on canvas. 32.3 × 46 cms. Paris, Musée d'Orsay.

**60** Degas, Study for *The Dance Rehearsal Room: Two Dancers*, *c*. 1871–2. *Essence*. 22.3 × 28.3 cms. Rotterdam, Boymans-van Beuningen Museum. CAT. 40

was changed while the painting was in progress. And the function of fixing poses conventionally granted to 'pure' drawing media such as pencil or chalk was here superseded by an experimental medium, *essence*, which conveniently fused the qualities of painting and drawing.

Degas was particularly keen on the motif of dancers at the bar, which occurs as early as *The Dance Rehearsal Room* of 1872 and continues at least to the turn of the century. Work at the bar was the second standard exercise a dancer had to follow daily, after half-an-hour's painful practice at keeping the feet turned out and parallel (*se tourner*). Next the dancer clasped the ankle of a foot stretched straight to the waist-high bar, changing legs on a command and never ceasing to smile (*se casser*).[85] Degas seems to have admired the dancers for their submission to the private, rigorous discipline that was the essential preparation for the seemingly effortless grace displayed to the public in the ballet. The dance rehearsal formed a sympathetic parallel to his own beliefs as an artist, founded on constant study of the paradigms and rudiments of his own art, while the dancer using the bar to steady herself in a strained posture was similar to a life model using straps and blocks to make a pose more tolerable and so possible for the artist to draw.

One of Degas's most powerful and complete pictures was composed on this theme about 1876–7: *Two Dancers at the Bar* (61). Its genesis via three very different drawings provides an excellent gauge of Degas's draughtsmanship at this time. The first of these seems to have been a black chalk drawing executed with some rapidity, no doubt because the pose was hard to hold (62). It is very much a working sheet, on which he made a number of adjustments to the upper half of his figure, altering contours and shifting the arms to allow a greater flow from left elbow to right wrist, the points of tension. He made a further drawing, now more obviously intended for a composition, in *essence* on green prepared paper (78). Brushed with great virtuosity, a fluid wash of *essence* was worked over a drier, coarser mixture, in an unusual harmony of lavender and sharp green. He used a fingerprint to create texture behind the right figure's ear, and smeared the black he used for her hair with a rag. Her pose was refined by raising the head slightly, to give an unbroken undulation across her shoulders. The left-hand dancer is less substantial in her uncomfortable pose, except for the extended leg. To remedy this Degas had recourse to a further drawing, this time in pencil (63). He retained the arm holding the bar under her bust but lowered the other to grip the bar, turning her head in profile to the right. In another sketch on the same sheet he made sense of her supporting leg, and in yet another he made final adjustments to the out-

**61** Degas, *Two Dancers at the Bar*, *c.* 1876–7. Essence. 75.6 × 81.3 cms. New York, The Metropolitan Museum of Art, Bequest of Mrs H. O. Havemeyer, 1929. The H.O. Havemeyer Collection

stretched arm of the right-hand figure. Evidently this sheet was on hand as he painted the final picture, for the pigment splashes on it tally with colours used in *Two Dancers at the Bar*. This extraordinary painting, probably shown at the 1877 Impressionist exhibition, is very much the result of draughtsmanly researches. It owes its adventurous equilibrium to Degas's preparation of the figures in advance; his calculated risk with the canvas's *mise-en-page* was a problem of space, not of form. Concentration on the essentials of the pose, rhythm and volume of his figures in

drawings must have led Degas's interest away from the high finish of the ballet subjects, such as *The Dance Rehearsal Room*, on which he had been working only a few years previously, and this would be of great import for his later work. The one detail he did employ in *Two Dancers at the Bar* was by no means superfluous – the watering can. It served a threefold purpose: as plausible accessory used to sprinkle floors to dampen dust and skiddy patches, as an essential counterweight in the compositional gravity, and as a cheeky echo of the right-hand dancer's pose.

48

**63** Degas, Study for *Two Dancers at the Bar*, *c*.1876–7. Pencil. 30.9 × 19.5 cms. New York, Mr and Mrs William R. Acquavella. CAT. 49

**62** Degas, Study for *Two Dancers at the Bar: Dancer from behind*, *c*.1876–7. Black chalk. 31.1 × 20 cms. Paris, Musée du Louvre, Cabinet des Dessins. CAT. 47

**64** Degas, Copy after Mantegna, *Calvary*,
*c*.1868–9. Oil on canvas. 69 × 92.5 cms.
Tours, Musée des Beaux-Arts. CAT. 36

**65** Degas, *Sheet of Studies*, 1858–9. Pencil, pen and ink,
with green, brown, and pale blue washes. 30.5 × 23.5 cms.
The Cleveland Museum of Art. CAT. 10

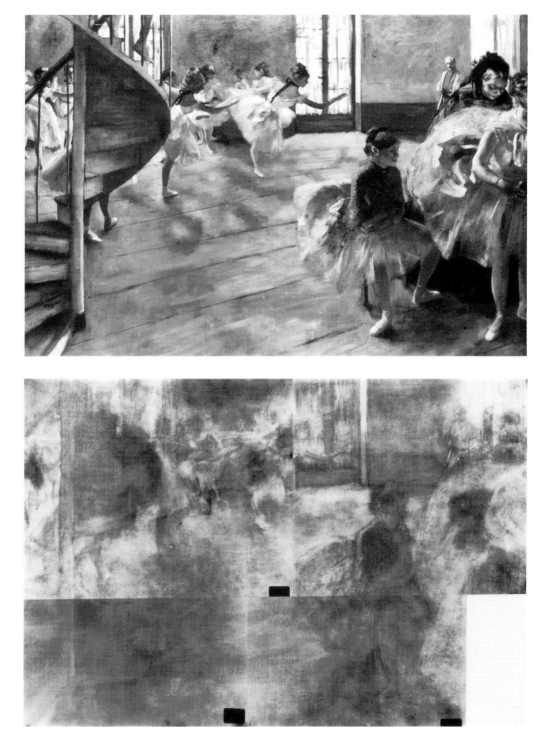

**66** Degas, *The Rehearsal*, 1873–4. Oil on canvas. 58.4 × 83.8 cms. Glasgow, The Burrell Collection. CAT. 44

**67** X-ray of no. 66

'One must contrive to give the impression of nature by false means; but it must appear true.'

Degas.[86]

Unorthodox variety of media and preparatory procedures were the means by which Degas produced ballet pictures in the 1870s. If all the preliminary drawings for the *Dance Class* of 1873 (Washington, Corcoran Art Gallery), such as *Dancer adjusting her Shoulder Strap* (154), were in *essence*,[87] the same consistency by no means applied to the slightly later reworking of the theme, *The Rehearsal* (66).[88] In two black chalk drawings for figures on the right of the picture (69, 70) Degas surely had their interrelationship in mind, for the sheet of the dancer includes an indication of the maternal figure behind her, and vice versa. Above these two figures is the ballet-master Perrot, painted not from a calculatedly interlocking drawing but from a daguerreotype taken in St Petersburg some years earlier (68). Although flatteringly rejuvenated by Degas's brush, the figure of Perrot was described by de Goncourt in his *Journal* as 'the vulgar repoussoir of a ridiculous dance master.'[89] X-rays of the canvas (67) suggest that he was introduced as a second thought, with Degas painting out a column and reducing the strong light that were initially in the upper right corner. It was perhaps the result of working at one moment from a drawing and the next from a photograph that inadvertently provoked the abrupt spatial disengagement between Perrot and the nearer figures. Balancing the stacked arrangement of figures to the right, Degas fixed the left side with a spiral staircase, masking a mêlée of dancers. In the centre

68 C. Bergamasco, *Jules Perrot*, *c.*1860. Daguerreotype. Mr David Daniels.

69 Degas, Study for *The Rehearsal*, 1873–4. Black chalk. 47.5 × 30 cms. New Orleans, Isaac Delgado Museum of Art.

70 Degas, Study for *The Rehearsal*, 1873–4. Black chalk, heightened with white. 34 × 29 cms. Location unknown (Vente II, no. 356).

**71** Degas, *Les Amateurs (Paul Lafond and Alphonse Cherfils examining a Painting)*,
*c.*1878–80. Oil on panel. 28 × 36 cms.
The Cleveland Museum of Art. CAT. 59

72  Degas, *The Young Spartans Exercising*, c.1860–1.
Oil on board. 21 × 28 cms.
Cambridge, Mass., Fogg Art Museum. CAT. 20

two dancers rehearse the *arabesque* position, and the overall structure of *The Rehearsal* distantly recalls that of *The Young Spartans*. It differs from the history painting in that it relies on improvisation as much as on its earlier variant and preparatory drawings. *The Rehearsal* reveals an artist prepared to use a photograph as he would a preliminary study, who will sign and sell a painting which is resolved, even if it is unfinished by the standards of the day. For *pentimenti* are plainly visible, there are obvious exaggerations such as the outstretched arms of the *arabesque* figures, and the dancers along the rear wall are merely nebulous presences. But this improvisation, this sense of decisions being made on the canvas, is almost calculated to add to the image's spontaneity. The unfinished nature of the background figures eases one's perception of the dancers as they move through their *arabesques*; as we follow their motion adjacent forms are blurred. Here we have Degas, an artist capable of high finish, stopping short of it, modifying his skills of composition and execution the better to evoke instantaneous movement in a light-soaked room.

Nowhere in his career does Degas seem to have cast himself further adrift from the heritage of past art in which he had been trained than in the 1870s. Yet the lessons he had learned still run as a gentle current in his work at this time. Indeed, the ballet pictures throw light on the probable interests that determined some of his earlier copies. In the copy after Raphael's *School of*

**73** Degas, Copy after Raphael, *School of Athens*, *c*. 1853. Pencil. 23 × 15 cms. Oxford, Ashmolean Museum. CAT. 1

*Athens* (73) the young Degas investigated Raphael's solution for the interrelationship of two figures, emphasizing a narrative connection between them by gesture and the almost mirror-like repetition of their poses, using the device of *contraposto*, which twists the head in contrary direction to the impetus of the body.

**76** Degas, *Two Dancers, Harlequin and Colombine*, c.1895. Charcoal. 27.8 × 23 cms. Rotterdam, Boymans-van Beuningen Museum. CAT. 89

Some twenty years later such devices were an instinctive element of his mature repertoire, and in the exciting oil sketch *Two Dancers on Stage* (79) he used a similar solution. As the right-hand dancer gestures entreatingly, the other figure, in a *contraposto* pose that implies her momentarily frozen impulsion, moves off into the open space which dominates the left half of the image. The *contraposto* supplies movement, and the space suggests the passage of time, for in a moment the fleeting dancer will fill it. Another

**74** Engraving after Raphael, *School of Athens*, 27.7 × 25 cms. From W. Ottley, *The Italian School of Design . . .*, London, 1823, between pp. 50–1. Oxford, Ashmolean Museum.

**75** Degas, *Two Dancers, Harlequin and Colombine*, c.1890–5. Oil on panel. 33 × 23.5 cms. Paris, Musée d'Orsay.

OPPOSITE
**77** Degas, *The Duet (The Singing Rehearsal)*, *c*.1868–70. Oil on canvas. 81 × 65 cms. Washington, Dumbarton Oaks Research Library and Collection. CAT. 38

**78** Degas, Study for *Two Dancers at the Bar*, *c*.1876–7. *Essence.* 47 × 62.5 cms. London, British Museum. CAT. 48

**79** Degas, *Two Dancers on Stage*, *c*.1874. Oil on paper. 16.8 × 21.8 cms. USA, private collection.

twenty years further on, this kind of relationship still stimulated Degas. In a group of charcoal drawings from the mid-1890s, which are probably reworkings of a slightly earlier, rather Watteau-esque painting (75) of *Harlequin and Colombine* (76), he placed the 'male' figure (actually posed by a female dancer) in a supplicatory position. Colombine responds in an orthodox *contraposto* pose, head turned towards Harlequin but torso twisted timorously away, perfectly attuned to convey both the rhythm and the narrative of the composition.

The pictorial possibilities that might be thrown up by copying old master art and then developed at a later remove can be inferred from Degas's fascination with Mantegna's *Calvary* (2).[90] It would be injudicious to suggest too direct or conscious links between the Mantegna and Degas's own work, or to deny that he drew visual ideas from elsewhere, but one can hypothesize about how a painting that held such consistent interest for Degas provoked pictorial issues in his mind. In the mid-1850s he had copied one of the standing soldiers dicing for Christ's garments, studying the drapery in rather pedantic fashion (80). He set the soldier, with his head turned actively away from the sinuous grace of the body, within its compositional context by lightly indicating the adjacent figures. These interests were again to the fore about 1874–5 when he drew Jules Perrot from life in order to feature him in *The Dance Class* he was then reworking (81, 82).[91]

80 Degas, Copy after Mantegna, *Calvary: Roman Soldier*, *c*.1853–5. Pencil and black chalk. 30.8 × 21.6 cms. Williamstown, Sterling and Francine Clark Art Institute. CAT. 4

81 Degas, *The Dancer Jules Perrot*,
*c.*1874–5. Charcoal and black chalk,
heightened with white. 48.4 × 30.5 cms.
Cambridge, Fitzwilliam Museum. CAT. 45

82 Degas, *The Dance Class*, *c.*1874–5.
Oil on canvas. 85 × 75 cms. Paris,
Musée d'Orsay.

Both standing figures are stabilized by
the vertical staff which offsets the irregu-
larity of their stance, and Perrot's head
is vividly screwed away from the central
axis of his body. The *Calvary* also includes two figures cut off at the bottom,
there to imply life outside the picture
space as much as to establish the foreground plane. During the 1870s Degas
frequently exploited this device, as in
his print *On Stage I* (85), in which the
heads of the musicians and audience
protrude into our line of vision, placing
us too in the stalls. However, such a
practice was a commonplace in the popular imagery of the period,[92] and we are
reminded how much at this period Degas
pillaged journalistic illustration and caricature for pictorial ideas in order to add

**83** Degas, *Ballet Dancer with arms crossed*, 1872. Oil on canvas. 61.4 × 50.5 cms. Boston; Museum of Fine Arts. CAT. 42

**84** Degas, *Dancers Backstage*, 1872. Oil on canvas. 24.2 × 18.8 cms. Washington, National Gallery of Art. CAT. 41

a piquant modernity to his images of contemporary Paris. As the geneses of his pictorial devices and compositions become as complicated as this, we are driven to even greater respect for his capacity to assimilate visual possibilities from divergent sources into his highly personal art.

'I've never liked the reality of backstage.'
Jules Claretie, 1885.[93]

Degas's images of behind the scenes at the ballet represent a woman's world, viewed, or imagined, by a male artist. As well as those men who had connections in the theatrical world, it had long been customary for wealthy *abonnés* (or subscribers) to have access to the *foyer de danse* backstage at the Paris Opéra. A ballet dancer could make a prestigious mistress for a man of means trying to cut a dash in the Parisian *demi-monde*. Certainly the dancers were aware of this – one gossip of the period described Eugénie Fiocre trying to land an English milord[94] – and the mothers whom Degas included in such paintings as the Burrell Collection's *Rehearsal* and the Paris *Dance Class* (66, 82) lurked behind the scenes at the Opéra not so much to chaperone their daughters as to ensure that they found a suitably long-term and

lucrative lover, often a necessity to supplement the low income of a working-class family. Yet commentators at the time of Degas's interest in the society of the ballet regretted that backstage morality was less gamey than it had been, with dancers searching for security: 'They all have "someone", of course. A few have several "someones". But it's less for pleasure than out of necessity.'[95] Almost from the outset of his interest in the ballet Degas tackled the theme. For the irony of the Opéra, dedicated to the highest achievements of music and ballet, providing a hothouse in which sexual favours were bargained and bought across the class barrier can hardly have been lost on him. He began in 1872, a date that can be established thanks to a study of a dancer (86) made by his friend Evariste de Valernes, with an inscription indicating that it was made in a studio Degas left that year, only shortly after starting dance pictures.[96] Degas made a study of that model at the same session, from a more profile position, loosely worked in oil and setting a monochrome figure against a striking scarlet backdrop (83). He used the pose in a little painting about a third the size, *Dancers Backstage* (84). Here the dancer stands with a companion behind a bright green stage flat, poised in crafty self-containment against the blandishments of a top-hatted gentleman. This oil sketch was probably intended to be worked up into a larger painting; indeed, the monochrome dancer may have been the start of it, abandoned as a satisfying study. However, the idea seems not to have been pursued in a complete canvas for none of the similar compositions of exhibition status from this period, showing dancers behind a stage-flat, includes the man.[97] Nevertheless, he did not shrink on the grounds

86 de Valernes, *Ballet Dancer*, 1872. Oil on canvas. 55.5 × 46 cms. Inscr: '*Étude à peine commencée d'une/danseuse de l'opéra dans l'atelier/de mon ami Degas rue de Laval/ E. Valernes*'. Musée de Carpentras.

of propriety from showing such subjects. Some smaller variant, as yet unidentified, was shown at the Impressionist exhibition of 1877, where the critic Paul Mantz noted 'the young dancers with impoverished arms, the fat gentleman who strolls among these fairies and specializes in "protecting" debutantes . . . [Degas] understands all the blemishes of precocious vice; he sees the ugliness beneath the make-up and he could, if he wanted, be a formidable caricaturist.'[98]

Around 1880 a great opportunity to produce a revealing compendium of seedy backstage society arose when Degas planned to illustrate his friend

Degas

Ludovic Halévy's *The Cardinal Family*
with a series of monotypes. Halévy was
a librettist and Opéra *abonné* who knew
his subject well, but his book is a com-
pilation of anodyne stories about one
particular family, psychologically simple
and in terms of social criticism, neuter.
Degas adhered only loosely to the text.
He treated the opening sequence, in
which Halévy himself meets Mme Cardinal in the corridors of the Opéra, some
five times,[99] and tackled the similar
scene of a conversation between them
in a dressing room (87). If the compositions of these images look back to lithographs of the Romantic period (88)
both in their subject and even in their

**89** Degas, *The Conversation (Ludovic Halévy and Mme Cardinal)*, *c.*1880.
Monotype. 21.3 × 16 cms. The Cleveland Museum of Art. CAT. 66

intimate, off-centre pairing of the figures,
they mark a further step forward in
Degas's obsession with reworking the
same motif over again. This is especially
so as he was given to reworking the
second, fainter impression of a monotype
with pastel, allowing further development of the subject. Thus while one version representing Ludovic Halévy talking to Mme Cardinal (89) is a virtuoso

performance in dabbing the ink-covered plate to provide a range of tones and patterns, another similar version was animated with the application of pastel, particularly emphasizing Mme Cardinal's characteristic tartan rug (90). The Stuttgart version of *Ludovic Halévy and Mme Cardinal* (87) is the most resolved of three impressions[100] of this scene, Degas using only a limited range of colours to elaborate the setting and intensify the physiognomies he had already conjured up at the monotype stage. The series of monotypes for *The Cardinal Family* was never published – perhaps there were difficulties in the commercial reproduction of such images, perhaps Halévy found them inappropriate – but it does embody the fertility of Degas's art at this time. For with these monotypes he was attempting an ambitious suite of illustrations in an experimental medium, essaying further the possibilities of mixed media and repetitive development of images, and ploughing back into the field of popular imagery, from which he had drawn so much in the 1870s, his own, albeit ill-fated, illustrative contribution.

**90** Degas, *Ludovic Halévy talking to Mme Cardinal*, c. 1880. Pastel over monotype. 21.6 × 15.9 cms. Paris, J.-C. Romand.

'He's a curious observer who looks for himself and sees things others have never seen.'
Charles Bigot, 1877.[101]

Degas's art was founded on an acute consciousness of the actual act of looking, and was concerned to articulate this consciousness to the spectator. During the late 1860s and 1870s in particular, at the height of the Naturalist aesthetic with its determination to convey factual information about the quotidian world, Degas produced images of multifaceted complexity, images that simultaneously encourage us to be aware of how we perceive in our daily lives, and remind us that we are looking at the artifice of a picture.[102] Nor did he forget that we all acquire certain conventions for looking, just as he had done as a student. This whole net of interrelationships is encompassed in one of his racecourse paintings of the late 1860s and especially in its chief figure, *Woman looking through Field-glasses*, whom he studied in a number of remarkable drawings (91).[103] The painting was a studio contrivance developed from drawings but designed, with its cut-off forms and cantering horses, to give a sense of glimpsed immediacy. The woman with the field-glasses reminds us of the act of looking; we are the object of her gaze as she is of ours. Her pose is derived from the Antique sculpture *Pudicity* (92), one of the examples of ideal beauty Degas would have admired as a student. Yet if the way he was taught to see still had a residual effect, the *Woman looking through Field-glasses* may also owe to the more contemporary source of a stereoscopic daguerreotype (93).[104] Here too

91 Degas, *Woman looking through Field-glasses*, c.1866–8. *Essence* and black chalk. 31.4 × 19 cms. Glasgow, The Burrell Collection. CAT. 34

92 *Pudicity*, Roman, late 1st century AD. Marble. Height: 209 cms. Rome, Vatican Museums.

93 Anon., *Half-length portrait of a young lady with opera glasses*, c.1855. Stereoscopic daguerreotype. 6.5 × 5.5 cms (each frame). Private collection.

is a deliberate play with the act of look-ing, the viewer viewed through a device to give an illusion of three-dimensional-ity. This daguerreotype, at very least, points out that Degas's consciousness of visual perception was shared by con-temporaries, and his articulation of it was a combination of inherited conven-tion and individual observation.

Degas's extraordinary powers of ob-servation were widely recognized by the reviewers of the Impressionist exhi-bitions.[105] Indeed, so shrewd were his perceptions that the novelist Edmond de Goncourt, no mean observer himself, not only noted in his Journal of 1878 Degas's comment that 'one no longer sees society women with sloping shoulders', but three years later passed it off as one of his own aphorisms in a magazine column he wrote.[106] The late 1870s wit-nessed Degas's most intense experimen-tation with the means by which to articu-late his observations pictorially, as height-ened perceptions of the modern urban world. This is evident in his café-concert motifs. He had been an enthusiast for this vulgar and ebullient form of popular entertainment, the French equivalent of the music hall, at least since 1872, when he took his startled brother René to hear 'idiotic songs . . . and other stupid absurdities',[107] but it was not until 1876–8 that he produced a suite of works on the theme in a wide variety of media, oil and pastel, lithograph and monotype.[108] A number of these images were derived from sketches made while watching performances at café-concerts. He observed the singers' characteristic attitudes in speedily drawn sketches (95), sometimes as many as half-a-dozen per notebook page.[109] In some instances he followed the more usual path of select-ing the sketch that seemed to him best to provide a synthesis of the performance and then work it up into a finished image, as he did with both his highly unconventional oil on tile motif of a busty singer (97) and his sophisticated lithograph of *Mlle Bécat at the Café-concert des Ambassadeurs*, where her de-monstrative pose is spreadeagled under the illumination of gas light and fire-works (98). In other cases he seems to have realized, as a result of his initial

94 Degas, *Mlle Bécat at the Café-concert des Ambassadeurs: Three Motifs*, *c.*1877–8. Lithograph transferred from three monotypes. 29.1 × 24.3 cms. Bern, E.W. Kornfeld. CAT. 56

sketches, that the dynamic of a performance would be best represented by serial images. From his sketches he quickly improvised monotypes, and then transferred these images onto a lithographic stone, which he worked further.[110] The result is an almost cinematic sequence, catching Mlle Bécat's hunched, angular movements in a tripartite image intended to approximate more closely to a spectator's impression of the act than could a single image (94). Yet for all the innovatory experimentation of these café-concert scenes, they too appear to be underpinned by the conventions in which Degas had been trained to see or even by earlier poses designed for entirely different contexts.

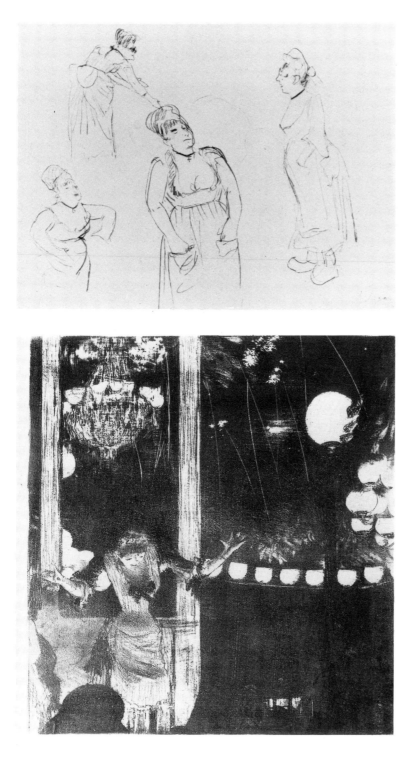

**95** Degas, *Sketches of a Café-concert Singer (Mlle Bécat)*, *c*.1875–7. Pencil. 26 × 35 cms. Nb.29, p.11. New York, Mr and Mrs Eugene Thaw.

**97** Degas, *Mlle Bécat aux Ambassadeurs*, *c*.1875–7. Oil on tile. 20.3 × 20.3 cms. Private collection. CAT.53

**96** Degas, *Café-concert Singer*, *c*.1876–7. Crayon lithograph. 25.2 × 19.2 cms. London, British Museum, Department of Prints and Drawings. CAT.54

**98** Degas, *Mlle Bécat at the Café-concert des Ambassadeurs*, *c*.1877–8. Lithograph. 20.5 × 19.3 cms. Bern, E.W. Kornfeld. CAT.55

**99** Degas, Copy after Le Sueur, *St Paul preaching at Ephesus*, *c*.1868–9. Oil on canvas. 41.3 × 33.3 cms. Kasmin Ltd. CAT. 37

**100** Degas, *Café-concert des Ambassadeurs*, *c*.1875–7. Pastel over monotype. 37 × 27 cms. Lyons, Musée des Beaux-Arts.

**101** Degas, *Standing Female Figure with Bared Torso*, *c*.1866–8. Essence. 47 × 30 cms. Basel, Öffentliche Kunstsammlungen. CAT. 35

A decade earlier Degas had copied Le Sueur's *St Paul Preaching at Ephesus* (99),[III] and this painting's orchestration of movement and gesture within an architectural, stage-like setting, establishing the dominant relationship of 'performer' over audience, seems to lie behind the composition of many of his café-concert motifs (100). It was also in the late 1860s that he executed a powerful *essence* study of a half-naked woman (101). Although this image might have served as a study for either *The Duet* (77) or the so-called *Interior* (1868–9; Philadelphia,

102 Degas, *Ordination Ceremony in the Cathedral at Lyons*, 1855. Oil on paper. 31.4 × 23.3 cms. Cambridge, Fitzwilliam Museum. CAT. 7

McIlhenny Collection) it was not used in any known painting. However, Degas did not forget this imploring pose, and ten years later adapted it in his images of the café-concert.

Degas recognized that looking does not just involve *what* one sees but from *where* one sees. His interest in the unorthodox point of view dated back as far as 1855 when, on a summer visit to Lyons, he produced a small painting of an ordination ceremony in the cathedral, executed from memory and jottings made in a notebook (102).[112] Eschewing a conventional, ground-level view which would have stressed liturgical and individual detail, he preferred to look down from a gallery, so bishop and ordinands form an anonymous pattern of authority and obedience within the still space of the cathedral. He frequently returned to this fascination with looking down in the later 1870s. This viewpoint involves challenging artistic problems such as foreshortening and it also makes implicit assumptions about the role of the spectator. In the fan *Dancers and Stage Scenery* we are in a position – a stage technician's post perhaps – to peer between the flats to the dancers awaiting their cue (137). Such a viewpoint exposes the artifice of the performance; it does not allow us, like a spectator in the stalls, to suspend our disbelief. The several views from boxes Degas made around

103 Degas, *A Ballet from an Opera Box*, *c.*1880–3. Pastel. 55 × 48 cms. Paris, Durand-Ruel Collection.

this time are even more explicit. An image like *A Ballet from an Opera Box* (103) shows the dancer, bowing, seen from the privileged vantage of a box in which a well-groomed woman sits. Our viewpoint is that of her male escort standing behind her. Hence the spectator's angle of view does more than transcribe a plausibly naturalistic glimpse, but implies class and gender roles as well.

Degas's celebrated prints of *Mary Cassatt at the Louvre*, intended for *Le Jour et la Nuit*, an ill-fated album of prints on which he was collaborating in 1879–80, are more than technical *tours de force* in which he reworked the images in state after state.[113] They represent the act of looking, and relate to assumptions about how women look at art. It was commonplace in French iconography to imply that women had no real appreciation of art, as well as to use the objects

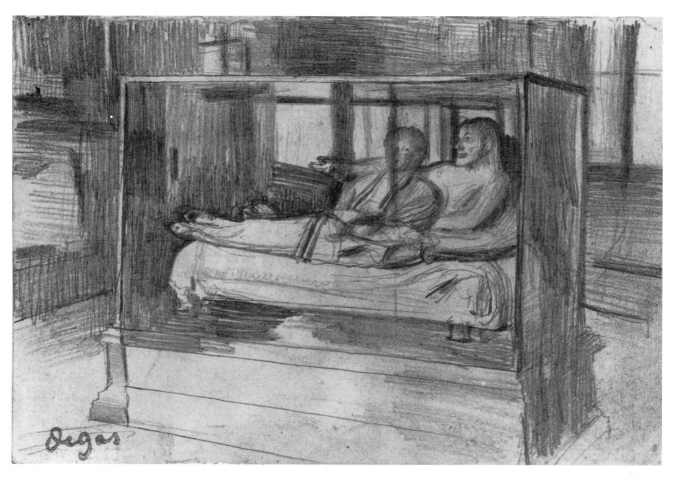

**105** Degas, *At the Louvre: the Etruscan Sarcophagus*, *c.*1879. Pencil. 10.5 × 16.5 cms. Williamstown, Mass., Sterling and Francine Clark Art Institute. CAT. 63

OPPOSITE
**104** Degas, *Mary Cassatt at the Louvre: The Etruscan Gallery*, *c.*1879–80. Softground etching, drypoint, aquatint and etching. 26.7 × 23.2 cms. Rotterdam, Boymans-van Beuningen Museum. CAT. 64

**106** Degas, *A Visit to the Museum*, *c.*1880–2. Oil on canvas. 90.2 × 67 cms. Boston, Mass., Museum of Fine Arts.

at which the female figures look to convey meanings about the spectators. About 1879 Degas copied in a notebook an Etruscan sarcophagus in the Louvre, carefully ruling the lines of the display case and recording the reflections in the glass (105).[114] He used the sarcophagus of a husband and wife in one of his prints of Cassatt at the Louvre (104), and in the background of a painting that also dates from this period, *A Visit to the Museum* (106), Degas included another image of marriage, Veronese's *Wedding at Cana* (Paris, Louvre). It was at this period that the middle-aged Degas was regretting that he was unmarried, telling

79

friends he was worried a wife would not understand his work.[115] He explained to Walter Sickert that *A Visit to the Museum* was meant 'to give the idea of that bored and respectfully crushed and impressed absence of all feeling that women experience in front of paintings',[116] and in the prints of Cassatt Degas seems to imply that she is more conscious of her suave posture than aesthetic experience.

In Degas's sophisticated images about looking the spectator is usually made to see from the position of a cultivated, upper middle-class male. Orthodox patriarchal prejudices lurk not far beneath the surface.[117] Whether the spectacle is construed through the prism of past art, regarded from a privileged point of view, or invokes assumptions about others' capacity to look, for Degas, observation was inseparable from ideology.

### 'Here's a really new initiative, an attempt at realism in sculpture.'
Charles Ephrussi, 1881.[118]

The catalogue of the 1880 Impressionist exhibition promised a *Little Dancer of Fourteen Years (Statuette in wax)* from Degas, but no such sculpture appeared. It was shown the following year, and was generally admired for its technical accomplishment and innovative ambition, though some found the subject of the young dancer and her saucy mien shocking.[119] Modelled in wax, the original sculpture (Upperville, Virginia, Mellon Collection) has an eerily lifelike sheen only partially conveyed by later bronze casts (110). Not content with modelling

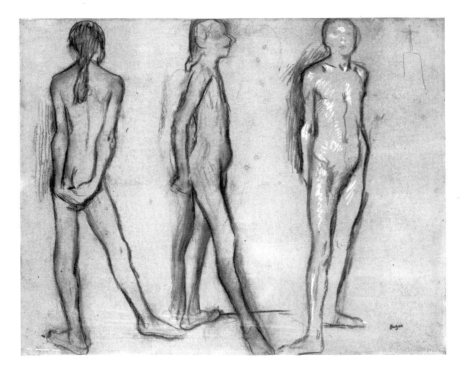

the flesh and features with extraordinary accuracy, Degas clothed his figure, two-thirds life-size, in a real tutu and ballet slippers, giving her a wig of horsehair tied in a satin ribbon. The shock of its realism is hardly dulled today. The *Little Dancer* was not Degas's first sculpture,[120] but it may well have been his first figure piece. It is uncertain how Degas's work on this ambitious project actually progressed. One view holds that he began with drawings of his nude model Marie van Goethem (who was fourteen in 1878), following these with a wax *maquette* (107, 108). Then came the drawings of her clothed (109) and the final sculpture.[121] Another view subtly suggests that the drawings of Marie in this pose – half-a-dozen sheets with sixteen different views of her – resulted from exercises that Degas set himself in a notebook, planning to draw the

**107** Degas, Studies for *Little Dancer of Fourteen Years*, c.1878–80. Charcoal, heightened with white. 48 × 63 cms. Private collection. CAT. 68

**108** Degas, Nude Study for *Little Dancer of Fourteen Years*, c.1878–80. Bronze. Height: 71.8 cms. Edinburgh, National Gallery of Scotland. CAT. 69

same figure from above and below, from mirror reflections, from all angles.[122] The realization of a three-dimensional version of the pose came as a logical development of these studies.[123] However, from the very outset of his career Degas had drawn the same form from a number of angles. Frequently this involved sculpture, as in a sheet he made

in black and red chalk after the Classical *Borghese Warrior* (111, 112), whose back he drew from three viewpoints.[124] He had also made *têtes d'expression*, academic studies of typical facial expressions, in the same way.[125] Again, drawing a figure from an unusual angle or in a mirrored pose was characteristic of his studio practice in the late 1870s – as witnessed

**109** Degas, Studies for *Little Dancer of Fourteen Years*, *c.*1878–80. Black and brown chalk and pastel. 47.2 × 58.8 cms. London, private collection. CAT. 70

**110** Degas, *Little Dancer of Fourteen Years*, *c.*1878–81. Bronze, with pigmented tarlatan skirt and dyed silk bow. Height: 99.1 cms. University of East Anglia, Robert and Lisa Sainsbury Collection. CAT. 72

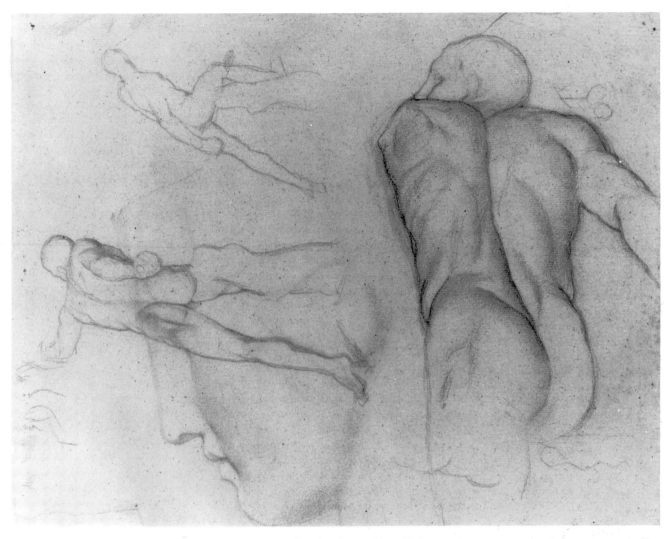

112 Degas, Copy after *The Borghese Gladiator*, *c.*1854–6. Black and red chalk. 31.1 × 24.1 cms. Williamstown, Mass., Sterling and Francine Clark Art Institute. CAT. 6

111 *The Borghese Gladiator*, *c.*100 BC. Marble. Length: 199 cms. Paris, Musée du Louvre.

by the studies for *Diego Martelli* (27, 29) and of *Two Dancers* (148) respectively – and he scarcely needed to produce such a consistent group as the drawings of Marie van Goethem simply as an exercise. For a new and challenging project, he judiciously reverted to conventional means of preliminary life drawing.

We do not know what was Degas's purpose in executing the *Little Dancer*. But a pattern appears when one takes into account other instances around 1880 when Degas drew the same figure several times 'in the round', such as three sheets of café-concert singers or two of a woman putting on her corset,[126] as well as the small contemporaneous statuette of the *Schoolgirl*, studied from several points of view in notebook drawings.[127] All of these, in whatever medium, are images of Parisiennes, co-ordinating pose, gesture and physiognomy into the representation of the characteristic type: in the case of the *Little Dancer*, the gauche grace and pubescent cockiness of the ballet girl. Studying both sculpture and facial expression from multiple viewpoints was a throwback to his earliest practice, as was his return to drawing from life. In all probability the *Little Dancer* was the only fully resolved example of a series of projected sculptures, a scheme aborted because making sculpture was too slow a process given the high standard of naturalism Degas had set himself.

## 'It's been my lifelong dream to paint walls.'

Degas, quoted by Vollard.[128]

Late in life Degas expressed his regret at never having executed any murals or other decorative paintings. This may seem paradoxical given the generally modest scale of his mature work and his Impressionist concern for the spontaneous, but it is in fact most understandable. As a student he had studied the fresco painters of the Italian Renaissance, including Benozzo Gozzoli's *Journey of the Magi* and Michelangelo's *Last Judgement* (123, 120), as well as contemporary decorations such as the religious murals of Hippolyte Flandrin.[129] For an artist in nineteenth-century France a commission to decorate a public building was a matter of great prestige. Indeed several of Degas's former student colleagues such as Bonnat, Delaunay, Emile Lévy and Puvis de Chavannes were involved in the decoration of the Panthéon, begun in the 1870s, while in the following decade younger friends such as Henry Lerolle, Georges Jeanniot, John Lewis-Brown and Albert Besnard were em-

ployed in the renovation of the Hôtel de Ville. Critics had consistently recognized the decorative qualities of Impressionism,[130] and Degas's fellow members of the Impressionist circle had planned or undertaken decorative schemes: Renoir for the publisher Charpentier in 1876, Monet for Hoschedé at Montgéron in 1876–7 and Manet for the Hôtel de Ville in 1879.[131] In mid-career, Degas was certainly thought of as a potential decorator. Gustave Geffroy argued forcibly in 1886 that a ceiling or mural decoration should be commissioned from Degas, repeating this appeal in 1894.[132]

However, Degas did take active, albeit unresolved, steps towards decorative schemes, and to a greater extent than has been recognized. Some of these projects appear to have overlapped with his sculptural interests, for the pastel inscribed 'Portraits in a frieze for the decoration of an apartment'[133] shown at the 1881 Impressionist exhibition shares the subject of the female Parisian type with the *Little Dancer* and *Schoolgirl* sculptures, while the magnificent *Frieze of Dancers* (114) is a painting on a decorative scale which sees the figure in the round as Degas's 'sculptural' drawings do.[134] Other projects related directly to his concerns as a painter. Apart from some very early ideas,[135] these date from around 1880. Prior to the pastel exhibited in 1881, he had shown the untraced tempera painting *Essai de décoration* at the 1879 Impressionist exhibition. Typically, his interests involved the study of past art, and in a letter of 1883 he urged his friend Rouart, then visiting Venice, to reconnoitre Tiepolo's frescoes in the Palazzo Labia.[136] It may well be that Degas's painting on tile of the café-concert singer (97) was related to decorative ideas, for Mme Bracquemond had

**114** Degas, *Frieze of Dancers*, c.1895. Oil on canvas. 70 × 200 cms. The Cleveland Museum of Art.

designed a decoration in faïence tile panels, the cartoons for which had been exhibited at the 1879 Impressionist show, and Renoir and Pissarro had been experimenting with painting on cement, perhaps to simulate the appearance of fresco.[137] The techniques of fresco painting were discussed by Degas's close colleagues Pissarro and Zandomeneghi about 1882, and it is difficult to imagine him not participating in these conversations.[138]

A sketch in a notebook, made about 1879 (113), set in train an obsession with a series of ballet rehearsal room pictures on which Degas worked off and on until the early 1900s.[139] The forty-odd variants all measure some 40 by 90 centimetres, a horizontal frieze-like format, with two-thirds of the canvas a shallow space

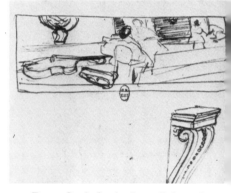

**113** Degas, Study for the *Dance Rehearsal Room* series, c.1879. Pencil. 16.7 × 11.1 cms. Nb. 31, p. 70. Paris, Bibliothèque Nationale.

**115** Degas, *Dancer adjusting her Tights*, c.1880–5. Black chalk, heightened with white, over pencil. 24.2 × 31.3 cms. Cambridge, Fitzwilliam Museum. CAT. 77

116 Degas, *Dancers in the Rehearsal Room, with a Double Bass*, *c.*1879–85. Oil on canvas. 39 × 89.5 cms. New York, Metropolitan Museum of Art. CAT. 75

117 Degas, *Three Nude Dancers at Rest*, *c.*1900–5. Lithograph, retouched in black chalk and pastel. 19.5 × 26.8 cms. Bern, E.W. Kornfeld. CAT. 102

RIGHT
118 Degas, *Green Dancers*, *c.*1883. Pastel. 71 × 39 cms. Location unknown; *Pink Dancers*, *c.*1883. Pastel. 72 × 39 cms. Pasadena, Norton Simon Foundation. Repr. from Lafond, II, opp. p. 30.

backed by a gently receding wall, opening out to right or left into greater depth. Degas worked intensely on these motifs in the early 1880s, preparing figures for them in careful drawings (115) and reworking paintings. *Dancers in the Rehearsal Room with a Double Bass* (116), for instance, was probably begun about 1879 and then retouched in the mid-1880s.[140] The rare lithograph of *Three Nude Dancers at Rest* (117), heightened with chalk and pastel and pared down to the figures alone, must have been executed after 1900 given the casually revised elasticity of the contours.[141] There is some dispute about whether these horizontal compositions were intended as decorative schemes or not.[142] Surely they must have been. The shallow space, uninsistent echoing of poses and

subdued colour range, as well as their panel-like format, would have suited them well to an architectural location. Paired with another subject – say one of the equestrian friezes of identical size (128) – whose composition opened out in the other direction, these designs would have made ideal decorations flanking a door. That Degas conceived of images as decorative pairs is apparent from two pastels of about 1883, *Green* and *Pink Dancers* (118). Not only do they echo each other's pose and harmonize with each other's colours, but they too are of almost identical size.[143] Yet they went to different collectors and never seem to have hung together.[144]

It was also in 1879 that Degas undertook another project which can be linked to decoration. In January that year

119 Degas, *Miss Lala at the Circus
Fernando*, 1879. Oil on canvas.
117 × 77.5 cms. London, National Gallery.

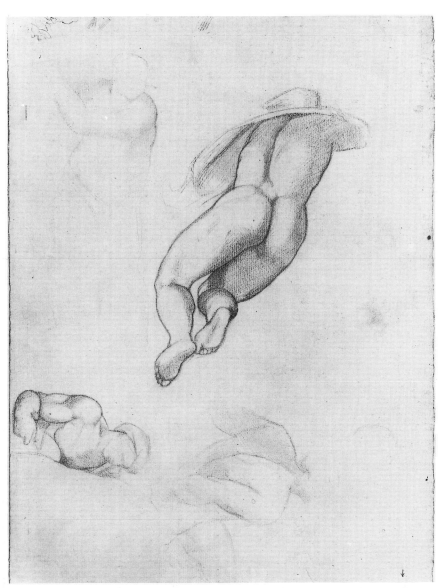

120 Degas, Copy after Michelangelo, *Last Judgement*, c. 1854–6. Pencil. 31.5 × 23.1 cms. Bremen, Kunsthalle. CAT. 5

121 Diaz, *The Assumption*, c. 1851. Oil on canvas. 39.2 × 27.4 cms. Baltimore, Walters Art Gallery.

those he made after Michelangelo's *Last Judgement* (120), Degas had studied the virtuoso draughtsmanship needed to represent anti-gravitational figures in the mural and ceiling paintings of the Renaissance, and he applied these lessons to the vertiginous image of *Miss Lala*. It may even be that he conceived the painting as a decorative motif, for the oil and pastel study is on a canvas exactly the same size as the frieze-like dance rehearsal rooms, and an earlier pastel of Lala used a yellow and pale blue harmony characteristic of Tiepolo.[145] His depiction closely parallels the traditional representation of the Assumption of the Virgin, recently used by Diaz in a painting that came on the Paris art market in 1878 (121).[146] *Miss Lala* was perhaps

he made a large number of notebook sketches, drawings and pastels of Miss Lala, an acrobat currently performing at the Circus Fernando. He selected the part of her act when she was raised to the roof of the circus by a rope which she held in her teeth, and the final painted version was shown at the Impressionist exhibition that year (119). At one level *Miss Lala* typifies Degas's accurate reconstruction of how we see. In the excitement of the performance our eyes would follow the acrobat, and we would not be aware of the rest of the audience, whom he had originally included in an early study executed in oil and pastel (138). But *Miss Lala* is more than naturalist refinement. In early copies, like a vehicle to scorn academic colleagues such as Delaunay and Bonnat, who painted large *Assumptions* to decorate churches,[147] applying his abilities to execute such a commission to a modern subject naturalistically presented. And he would have savoured the ironic substitution of the Virgin by a mulatto acrobat.[148]

Why do Degas's decorative initiatives appear to have come to nothing more than private studies, repeatedly revised and never executed *in situ*? He told Vollard that he feared the insecurity of property tenure; one day his work might fall into unappreciative hands.[149] Certainly his propensity for keeping work in progress, for the sweet-and-sour delights of perfectionism, was a factor. Of course, he never courted official approval. When he was finally offered a commission for cartoons in the early twentieth century by Gustave Geffroy, then director of the Gobelins tapestry works and as good as his word, it was simply 'too late'.[150]

'De la Croix has the name of a painter.'
Degas, letter to Bartholomé, 1882.[151]

Degas's irresolution of his decorative ambitions was in fact characteristic of many of his projects around 1880: the unpublished illustrations for *The Cardinal Family*, the aborted journal *Le Jour et la Nuit*, the year's delay with the *Little Dancer of Fourteen Years*. Over the five years that spanned the turn of the decade he was involved in so many innovative projects – monotypes, sculpture, printmaking, illustration, fans – and under such pressure – to sell work, to organize Impressionist exhibitions – that he took on too much, a tendency his father had warned him about over twenty years before.[152] Degas's imagination had always been full of ideas, as Duranty acknowledged publicly in *The New Painting*,[153] but, as his family had been aware in the 1860s, this inventiveness hindered his capacity to complete a project.[154] During the early 1880s Degas seems to have undergone a personal crisis, apparent from his correspondence. He expressed it most clearly in a letter to Lerolle, written in 1884: 'If you were single, fifty years old (for the last month), you would know similar moments when a door shuts inside one . . . I have made too many plans, here I am, blocked, impotent. And then I have lost the thread of things. I thought there would always be enough time.'[155] Lonely and frightened by his poor sight, it was from this period that Degas began to earn his reputation for misanthropy. Having allowed his art to diverge along too many paths of ambition and experiment, he dedicated the final quarter century of his career to furious concentration.

## 'Aren't all beautiful things made by renunciation?'
### Degas.[156]

The theme of horse and rider was one to which Degas returned again and again from the outset of his career to about 1900.[157] A composition that he consistently favoured for these images was a frieze-like design. The many copies that he made as a student from casts of the Parthenon Frieze[158] schooled him in repetitive rhythms and overlapping figures in relief (122). While in Florence in 1859 he made several copies after Benozzo Gozzoli's *Journey of the Magi* frescoes, probably on the advice of Moreau, who had done so the year before.[159] In the most impressive of these Degas selected a section where the horizontal impetus is punctuated by two riders seen head on, and he accentuated the relief by darker shading (123, 124).

**122** Degas, Copy after the Parthenon Frieze, *c.*1853–4. Pencil. 23.5 × 30.2 cms. Bremen, Kunsthalle. CAT. 2

**123** Degas, Copy after Benozzo Gozzoli, *The Journey of the Magi*, 1859 or 1860. Pencil. 26.2 × 30.5 cms. Cambridge, Mass., Fogg Art Museum. CAT. 12

**124** Benozzo Gozzoli, *The Journey of the Magi*, *c*.1459. Fresco (detail). Florence, Palazzo Medici-Riccardi.

But whereas Moreau used the copies towards his own version of the *Journey of the Magi*, Degas planned modern subjects. Via notebook sketches[160] and English sporting prints he transformed his experience of Gozzoli into a major drawing, *At the Races* (125). Two highly finished horses establish the main plane, Degas then complicating the relief by

adding subsidiary figures. This drawing served as a sort of template for three paintings of race-course scenes in the early 1860s, the most important of which, *Course de Gentlemen* (126), was dated 1862.[161] Degas's preoccupation with this frieze-like design is evident from his reworking of this canvas some fifteen years later,[162] as well as from paintings

**125** Degas, *At the Races*, *c.*1860. Pencil. 34.9 × 48.3 cms.
Williamstown, Mass., Sterling and Francine Clark Art Institute. CAT. 16

126 Degas, *Course de Gentlemen*, 1862 (reworked later).
Oil on canvas. 48.5 × 61.5 cms. Paris, Musée d'Orsay.

**127** Degas, *Race Horses*, *c*.1875–8. Oil on panel.
32.5 × 40.5 cms. Private collection. CAT. 50

**128** Degas, *Landscape with Mounted Horsemen*, *c*.1895.
Oil on canvas. 39 × 89 cms. Mrs John Hay Whitney. CAT. 90

of the 1870s. The fascinating panel *Race Horses* (127) belongs within this continuum. It may have originated in the late 1860s, when it included a fence to the left and, in place of the steward in the centre, a horse and rider lifted from copies after Meissonier's *Battle of Solferino* (1863; Paris, Musée d'Orsay), which Degas made at that time.[163] These were overpainted in the mid-1870s, Degas adding the standing figure, the horse and jockey seen from behind and the rider they overlap. He thus gave depth to his frieze by cutting across it at right angles, almost exactly as in his copy after Gozzoli. The steward's red flag and the jockey at the left reining hard give *Race Horses* a narrative element – the false start – typical of the 1870s but which Degas later renounced.

Just as the 40 by 90 centimetre dance rehearsal canvases were concerned less with naturalism than the decorative distribution of form, so were Degas's horse-and-jockey motifs in the same horizontal format. This group was under way in the mid-1880s.[164] One of them, which (in its present incarnation) dates from a decade later, shows how he now counterpointed his frieze-like emphasis with a gentle diagonal, abandoning any pretence of realistic atmosphere for a warm decorative harmony (128). Degas brought new resources into play during the 1880s and 1890s. Although he had first modelled horses in the late 1860s it was only some two decades later that his sculptures began to share drawing's status in his compositional deliberations. The role

99

**129** Degas, *Three Jockeys*, *c*.1900. Pastel.
49 × 62 cms. Private collection.

**130** Degas, *Horse and Jockey (The End of
the Race)*, *c*.1883–5. Black chalk.
14.7 × 19.8 cms. Glasgow, The Burrell
Collection. CAT. 78

of sculpture in Degas's late work is still uncertain. To some extent it acted, as his sight failed, as a reassuringly tactile form of creation. Given his willingness to destroy and restart waxes, it may be that modelling was for Degas a three-dimensional means of drawing.[165] And the highly resolved sense of movement and balance in the pieces must suggest that Degas could appreciate them as works of art in their own right. From the evidence of his modelled horses, he did not necessarily use them as a matter

of course in preparing paintings and pastels. For example, *Three Jockeys* (129), a pastel of about 1900, can be traced back via an earlier pastel[166] to a group of drawings made in the mid-1880s which fixed the pose of the central horse and jockey[167] (130). These drawings seem to have been made from memory, to judge from the rather disproportionate legs, and even though during the 1880s Degas had modelled a more accurate and energetic version of this animal (131), it was the pose of the

131 Degas, *Horse with Lowered Head*, c.1883–90. Bronze. Height: 18.1 cms. Cambridge, Fitzwilliam Museum. CAT. 79

drawings on which the pastels were based. If Degas's early conception of equestrian compositions had been indebted to his copies after Gozzoli, even thirty years later he was still prepared to learn. Alert to the very first article in 1878 on Edward Muybridge's photographs of animals in motion,[168] he copied a number of these after the full publication of *Animal Locomotion* in 1887 (132, 133).[169] Inevitably, he adapted them to his own ends, copying one in a rich red chalk the better to produce a counterproof,[170] fascinated by the way new technology made it possible for him to study with such accuracy the motif he first copied from the Parthenon Frieze.

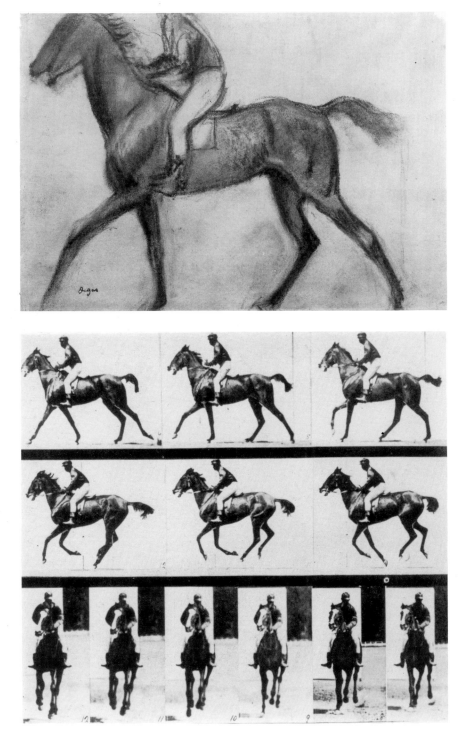

**132** Degas, *Race-horse and Jockey*, *c*. 1887–90. Red chalk. 28.3 × 41.8 cms. Rotterdam, Boymans-van Beuningen Museum. CAT. 81

**133** Muybridge, *Annie G. with Jockey* (.056 second). From *Animal Locomotion*, Pennsylvania, 1887.

'Art does not expand, it repeats itself.'

Degas, letter to Frölich, 1872.[171]

In his later career Degas elected to refine ideas he had explored earlier. An intriguing example of this occurs with a laundress motif. At the 1879 Impressionist exhibition he had shown an *essence* painting of *Two Laundresses* set against a schematic backdrop (134). With its physical concern for the distribution of weight and the almost mirrored pose, this 'frieze' might have been a study for one of the sculpted types he had in mind at that time. The motif resurfaced over twenty years later in a group of charcoal and pastel drawings,[172] the most monumental of which is *Two Laundresses with Horses* (135). The horses help set the figures in an enclosed, yet still relief-like, metropolitan space, and act as a

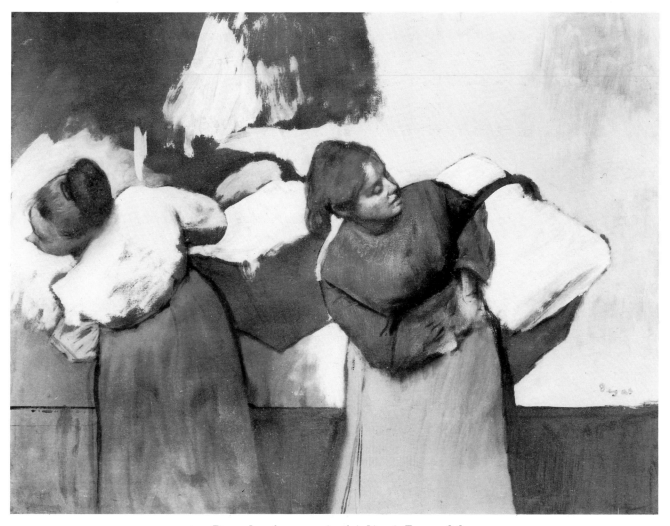

**134** Degas, *Laundresses carrying their Linen in Town*, c.1878–9.
*Essence*. 46 × 61 cms. Private collection. CAT. 58

135 Degas, *Two Laundresses and Horses*, *c*.1905. Charcoal and pastel. 84 × 107 cms.
Lausanne, Musée Cantonal des Beaux-Arts.

metaphor for the labouring laundresses. With its forceful charcoal strokes, sharp colour and additional strips of paper to give amplitude to the motif, *Two Laundresses with Horses* is characteristic of Degas's late work. So too is the continuity of concerns: the recycled poses, the forms in relief.

Another example of continuity is Degas's interest in posing the model in an almost symmetrical posture, often drawing this from an oblique angle to complicate a fundamentally simple structure. Symmetrical poses can be found in the 1860s – *Victoria Dubourg* (12) is a case in point – but they become an insistent part of the repertoire from the early 1880s. Then he used them in milliner subjects[173] and in studies for the horizontal dance rehearsals. *Dancer adjusting her Slipper* is one of these, a superb evocation of fatigue and harsh light falling on a glowing skin (136). The symmetrical pose was employed regularly

**136** Degas, *Dancer adjusting her Slipper*, *c.*1880–5. Pastel and charcoal. 49 × 62 cms. British Rail Pension Fund Works of Art Collection. CAT. 76

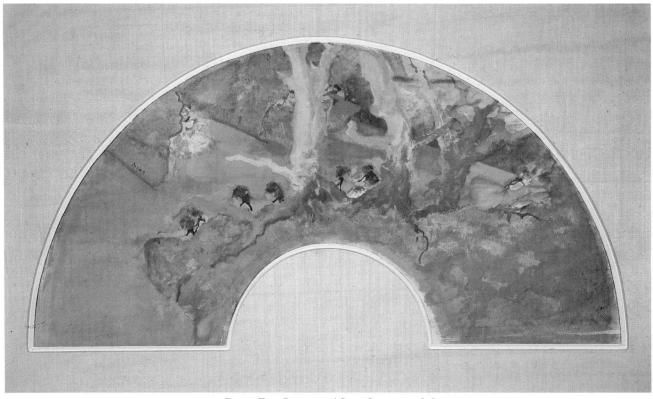

**137** Degas, Fan: *Dancers and Stage Scenery*, *c*.1878–9.
Gouache, with gold highlights. 31 × 61 cms.
Bern, E.W. Kornfeld. CAT. 57

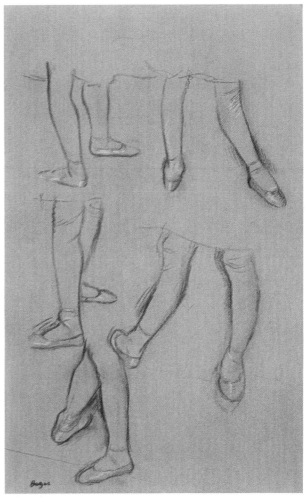

**138** Degas, Study for *Miss Lala at the Circus Fernando*, 1879. Oil and pastel on canvas. 89 × 39.5 cms. New York, Pierre Matisse. CAT. 62

**139** Degas, Studies for *Little Dancer of Fourteen Years*, c.1878–80. Pencil, charcoal and pastel on green paper. 48.5 × 30.5 cms. Thomas Gibson Fine Art Limited. CAT. 71

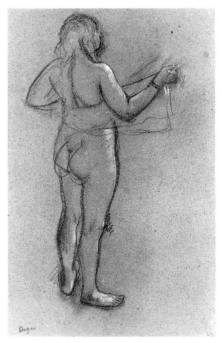

ABOVE LEFT
**140** Degas, *The Tub*, *c*.1880–3. Monotype.
42 × 54.1 cms. Paris, Bibliothèque d'Art et
d'Archéologie, Fondation Jacques Doucet.

ABOVE RIGHT
**141** Degas, *Study of a Nude Woman drying
herself with a Towel*, *c*.1880–3. Pencil,
heightened with white. 44.6 × 27.9 cms.
Oxford, Ashmolean Museum. CAT. 74

RIGHT
**142** Degas, *The Washbasin*, *c*.1880–3.
Monotype. 27.7 × 31.2 cms. Cambridge,
Fitzwilliam Museum. CAT. 73

143 Degas, *Woman at her Toilette*,
*c*.1880–3. Pastel over monotype.
43 × 58 cms. Pasadena, Norton Simon
Foundation.

for nudes. Featuring first in *scènes de toilette* such as *The Washbasin* of about 1880 (142), it has a plausible place in a naturalist environment. We stand taller than the woman, as if perhaps a client in a brothel watching a prostitute's preliminary – and necessary – demonstration of her personal hygiene. On the wall hangs a dress, consistent with Degas's reminder in a contemporaneous notebook to draw clothes 'which have just been taken off . . . and retain the shape of the body.'[174] He used a similar pose in a more ambitious monotype, *The Tub* (140). But prior to working up the second impression with pastel Degas drew the pose from life, recording both anatomy and fall of light with great exactitude (141, 143). By about 1900, when he returned to this generic pose, such precision was past. *Nude Standing beside a Chair* (144) emphasizes the contours, setting off the shapes of chin and breast against the extended elbows. Habitualized to this pose, Degas produced a schematic rather than observed image, investigating the fusion of muscular tension and physical bulk. He had studied the pose 'whole' in sculpture (145). The statuette added a forward momentum absent in the works on paper, but he

144 Degas, *Nude standing beside a Chair*,
*c*.1900–5. Charcoal. 91.4 × 66 cms. Private
collection. CAT. 101

145 Degas, *Dancer at Rest, Hands behind her
Back, Right Leg forward*. Bronze.
Height: 44.5 cms. London,
The Tate Gallery. CAT. 91

**146** Degas, *Landscape: Steep Coast*, *c*.1890–2. Pastel. 42 × 55 cms.
Geneva, Galerie Jan Krugier. CAT. 83

**147** Degas, *Woman having her Hair combed, c.*1884–6 (inverted). Pastel. 74 × 60.6 cms. New York, The Metropolitan Museum of Art, Bequest of Mrs H. O. Havemeyer, 1929. The H.O. Havemeyer Collection

does not appear to have employed this more dynamic alternative for the legs in pastels or charcoal drawings. One seated nude, posed symmetrically, shows Degas's imaginative capacity to metamorphose forms carried to its extreme. In the early 1890s he was engaged on a group of landscapes in pastel and monotype, which he composed from memory and *objets trouvés* such as piles of clothes or pebbles. They were exhibited in 1892, and *Landscape: Steep Coast* (146) probably dates from this time. Although at first sight it reads like a shoreline, this pastel was created from a version of *Woman having her Hair combed* (147), Degas transforming the female body into landscape forms like Zeus some unfortunate nymph.

If Degas's symmetrical poses seen from oblique angles complicated simplicity, elsewhere in his late work he

**148** Degas, *Two Dancers; c.* 1876–8,
*Essence.* 61.2 × 39.4 cms. New York,
The Metropolitan Museum of Art, Bequest
of Mrs H. O. Havemeyer, 1929. The H.O.
Havemeyer Collection

**149** Degas, *Two Dancers in Yellow*,
*c.* 1895–1900. Pastel. 60 × 42 cms. Private
collection. CAT. 98

was concerned to simplify complexity. No longer did he produce multi-figure compositions compiled from many poses as he had done in the 1860s and 1870s, but rather made more of a possibility essayed as long ago as *The Young Spartans*: the repetition and reversal of poses. By about 1890 his studio practice centred on the tracing of figures and designs, which allowed the motif to be synthesized, regrouped or reversed, and on counter-proofing (*contre-épreuve*), achieved by pressing an existing drawing onto a dampened sheet of paper to gain a reversed image that could then be worked up.[175] These were not entirely novel methods – Gericault and Daumier had both traced extensively[176] – and can be found in Degas's earlier work. As a student he used tracing for making copies, and in the mid-1870s had reversed ballet figures by these methods.[177] He had also employed mirrors for such drawings as *Two Dancers* (148) in which the same figure is seen in a reflection. Such methods were no longer occasional or experimental but habitual by the 1890s, when pastels such as *Two Dancers in Yellow* (149) were made. In a group of works on this theme Degas concentrated on two poses, not quite reflections but closely related, which act as a formal counterpoint not unlike the *Two Laundresses* (134).[178]

'Make a drawing, begin it again, trace it; begin it again, and trace it again'.
Degas.[179]

This obsession with the repetition of poses and compositions can also be found in the late work of Henner and Moreau. These colleagues of the 1850s returned, forty years on, to the pursuit of ideal form based on the synthesis of earlier ideas with which they had been inculcated as students. By the 1890s Degas no longer treated the dancer or bather as a type from the modern world but as one element in a formal arrangement, and his retreat to a studio-based refinement of a limited range of pictorial possibilities was to a large extent the consequence of his unmet ambitions as a painter of modernity. Yet his late work, for all his increasing alienation and poor sight, has a truly remarkable breadth and grandeur.

During the second half of the 1890s he worked tirelessly on variations of a ballet composition representing dancers

**150** Degas, *Four Dancers*, c.1895–1900. Oil on canvas. 150 × 180 cms. Washington, National Gallery of Art.

**151** Degas, *Half-length Dancer, adjusting her Shoulder Strap*, c.1895–1900. Charcoal and pastel. 47.5 × 37 cms. Bremen, Kunsthalle. CAT. 96

**152** *Diane de Gabies*, copy after Praxiteles. Marble. Height: 165 cms. Paris, Musée du Louvre.

beside a stage flat.[180] Based on a stock subject from the 1870s (84), this project culminated in a large canvas (150) and three highly finished pastels (168).[181] A multitude of charcoal and pastel drawings fuelled this enterprise, and it is all but impossible to establish exact inter-relationships as so many sheets were laid down and then dispersed following the posthumous sales of Degas's studio.[182] Typically, the project was both a rupture with and a continuation of the past. The motif of the figure adjusting a shoulder strap which he used so frequently (151) can be traced back to the Antique sculpture he admired and the life drawings he made as a student (152, 153). It had surfaced in studies for ballet pictures during the early 1870s (154), and remained in his imagination to be resuscitated. Another regular pose, the dancer turned away, arm upstretched, recollects a drawing made for the *Medieval War Scene* of 1865 (155, 156).[183]

**154** Degas, *Dancer adjusting her Shoulder Strap*, c.1873–4. Essence. 41.5 × 18 cms. Switzerland, private collection. CAT. 43

**153** Degas, *Standing Male Nude*, c.1856–8. Pencil. 28 × 20 cms. Paris, Durand-Ruel Collection.

**155** Degas, Study for *Medieval War Scene: Standing Female Nude*, *c*. 1865. Black chalk and stump. 39.3 × 22.5 cms. Paris, Musée du Louvre, Département des Arts Graphiques. CAT. 25

**156** Degas, *Half-length Female Nude*, *c.*1895–1900. Charcoal, heightened with white. 53.9 × 38.8 cms. Cambridge, Fitzwilliam Museum. CAT. 94

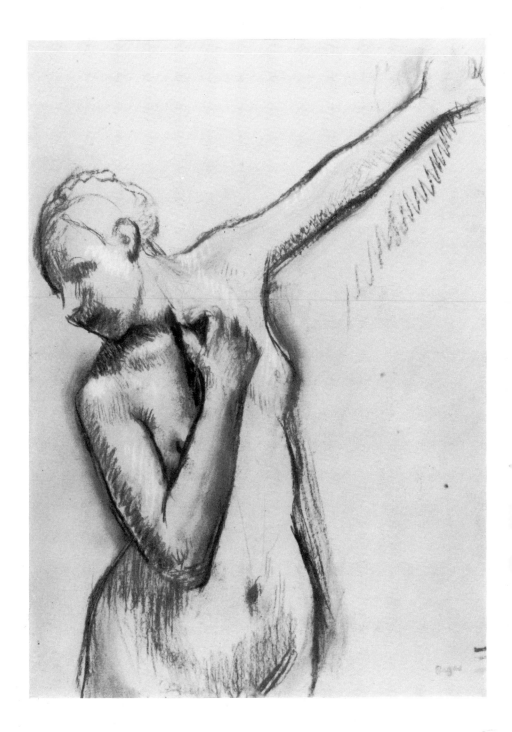

**157** Degas, Copy after Delacroix, *Entry of the Crusaders into Constantinople*, *c.*1859–60. Oil on paper. 35 × 38 cms. On loan to Kunsthaus, Zurich. CAT. 13

**158** Degas, *Nude drying her Hair*, *c.*1900. Charcoal and pastel. 77 × 75 cms. Lausanne, Musée Cantonal des Beaux-Arts. CAT. 100

**159** Degas, *After the Bath*, *c.*1905. Charcoal and pastel. 78 × 56 cms. The Columbus Gallery of Fine Arts, Ohio. CAT. 103

The Fitzwilliam's *Half-length Nude* appears, with its reworkings and capricious hatching, to have been drawn from life, yet it tallies closely, if not exactly, with one of a number of photographs which Degas used for this project (160–62). These photographs are a mystery; not necessarily taken by Degas, technical grounds suggest they may date as far back as the 1870s.[184] Other drawings approximate to their poses, but do not match. The Burrell Collection's *Dancer adjusting her Shoulder Strap* (165) may rather have been drawn from a statuette (163) that Degas must have made in connection with this project, given the somewhat generalized character of its articulation. Both of these drawings make use of shading in a way that gives relief to the figures, as Degas worked towards finished images with shallow space that have the effect of decorative polychrome bas-reliefs. Sculpture allowed a pose to be studied in the round, while counterproofing, like the negatives of his photographs, meant drawings could be reversed. There is a counterproof of the Burrell drawing,[185] and the multifigure design in the Whitworth Art Gallery was taken from a sheet now in Leningrad (164, 166), itself a resolved study for the upper section of one of

**160–2** Anon. (Degas?), Three Photographs of Dancers, *c*.1895 or earlier. Paris, Bibliothèque Nationale. CAT. 104

RIGHT
**163** Degas, *Dancer adjusting her Shoulder Strap*, *c*.1890–1900. Bronze. Height: 35 cms. Fridart Foundation. CAT. 92

the finished pastels.[186] It was by these often convoluted means that Degas compiled and corrected his compositions, and repetitious tracing and counterproof-

ing permitted multiple variants of pose and colour. Thus in the Leningrad drawing blue and red pastel dominates, while the Whitworth *contre-épreuve* was

165 Degas, *Dancer adjusting her Shoulder Strap*, *c*.1895–1900. Charcoal and pastel. 28 × 47 cms. Glasgow, The Burrell Collection. CAT. 95

OPPOSITE BELOW
164 Degas, *Study of Four Dancers*, *c*.1895–1900. Charcoal and pastel. 31 × 55 cms. Leningrad, Hermitage.

LEFT
166 Degas, *Study of Four Dancers*, *c*.1895–1900. Charcoal and pastel (counterproof). 45.4 × 64.5 cms. Manchester, Whitworth Art Gallery. CAT. 97

touched with yellow and orange. Preliminary drawing of these dancer motifs was usually in charcoal, highly suitable for Degas's duplicating processes. Those he worked up in pastel might be set aside at any stage, left monochrome (167), given an initial chromatic harmony (151), or carried through to high finish like the superb sheet from the Durand-Ruel collection (168), where the pastel, in rich, warm hues offset against a tart green, builds up by accretion, a studio-made coral reef.

'It is essential to do the same subject over again, ten times, a hundred times.'
Degas, letter to Bartholomé, 17 January 1886.[187]

In December 1891 Degas wrote to de Valernes: 'I am hoping to do a suite of lithographs, a first series on nude women at their toilette and a second one on nude dancers. In this way one continues to the last day figuring things out. It is fortunate that it should be so.'[188] His few dancer prints (117) relied on earlier ballet motifs; it was on the woman bathing that he concentrated attention, fascinated, as his letter suggests, by the apparently endless variation that could be worked on one essential pose. In August that year he had enthused about Delacroix's lithographs,[189] and in fact Degas's pivotal pose was lifted from the elder painter. About 1860, in preparation for his history painting *The Daughter of Jephthah* (1859–60; Northampton, Mass., Smith College Museum of Art), Degas had copied Delacroix's *Entry of the Crusaders into Constantinople* (157,

**169** Delacroix, *Entry of the Crusaders into Constantinople*, 1840. Oil on canvas. 410 × 498 cms. Paris, Musée du Louvre.

169).[190] Then Degas had vividly emulated Delacroix's touch as well as his colour, juxtaposing reds and greens with great verve. Thirty years later he returned to the grieving woman at the lower right, whom Cézanne had also admired,[191] retaining her broad back and tumbling hair but changing her setting from the melodramatic to the domestic. The initial lithographs were made in conjunction with a group of drawings such as the Williamstown *After the Bath* (171). In this sheet Degas orchestrated the body's rhythmic contours, develop-

ing a tonal balance between profile and mass which is closer to the later rather than the earlier states of the lithograph *Nude Woman standing, drying herself* (170, 172). Executed on tracing paper, the Williamstown drawing probably came at an intermediate stage in the development of the print, just as Degas had gone back to fresh drawings of established poses midway through *The Young Spartans*.[192]

Degas's irregular, improvisatory practice is evident in a large lithograph, *After the Bath*.[193] Combining the bending

**170** Degas, *Nude Woman standing, drying herself*, c.1891–2. Lithograph. 31 × 19.5 cms. London, British Museum. CAT. 84

**171** Degas, *After the Bath*, *c*.1891–2.
Charcoal. 35.2 × 25.1 cms. Williamstown,
Mass., Sterling and Francine Clark Art
Institute. CAT. 85

**172** Degas, *Nude Woman standing, drying
herself*, *c*.1891–2. Lithograph.
33 × 23.5 cms. Cambridge, Mass., Fogg Art
Museum. CAT. 86

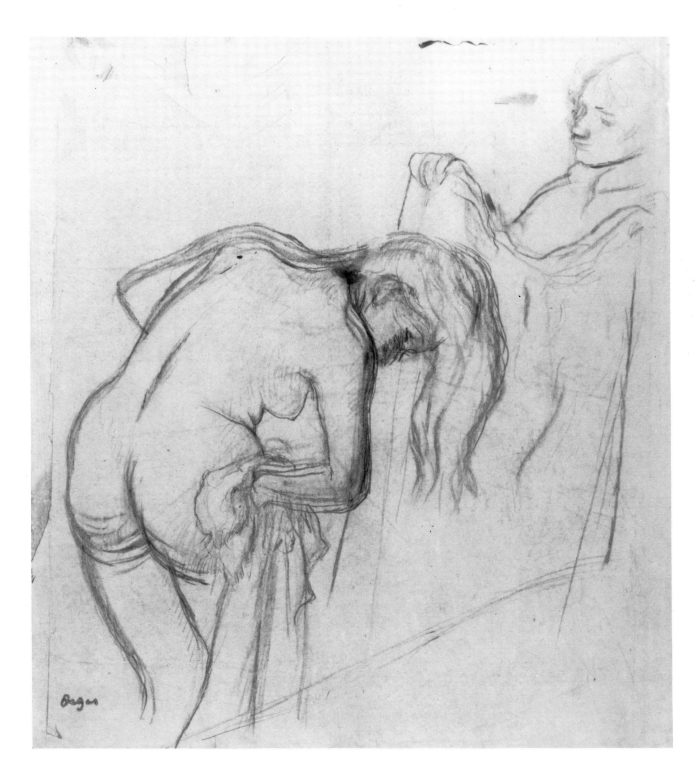

**173** Degas, *After the Bath (large version)*, *c.*1891–2. Lithographic crayon and pencil, and wash. 35 × 32.8 cms. London, British Museum. CAT. 87

**174** Degas, *After the Bath (large version)*, *c.*1891–2. Lithograph. 32 × 44.5 cms. The Art Institute of Chicago.

bather with a maid, this print began as a linear motif. Degas used pencil and wash over an early impression (173) to refine the contours: raising the shoulder, amplifying the buttocks, detailing the breast. The later impressions (174) then set the more sharply defined pose within

a richly textured setting with almost sculptural impact.

Degas's fascination with this pose continued long after his sequence of prints, all made in the early 1890s. The pose was altered from a woman wiping her hip to one drying her hair. This

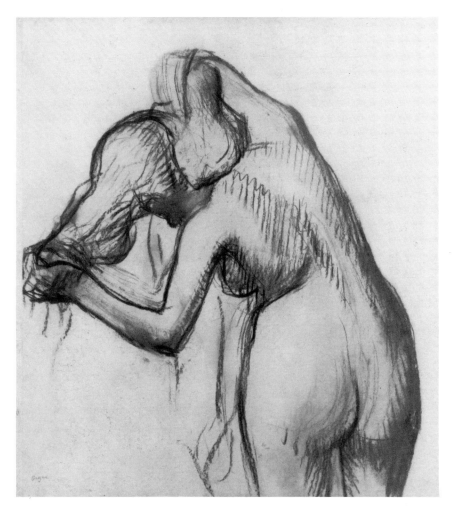

**175** Degas, *Female Nude drying her Neck*, *c*.1900. Charcoal. 79.3 × 76.2 cms. Cambridge, King's College (Keynes Collection). CAT. 99

sculptural form.[194] These repetitions of a single form were embellished with striking colour. The Lausanne pastel, apart from the ice-blue towel, is a medley of warm hues, while others are predominantly cool or harmonize extraordinary combinations of colour: apricot and lime-green, vermilion and violet. In these late pastels Degas surpassed even Delacroix in fusing energy of line and luminous colour.

**176** Degas, *Woman drying her Hair*, *c*. 1890–1900. Bronze. Height: 46 cms. Private collection.

balanced the complexity of action to one side of the figure against the unbroken undulation of the back, a solution closer to Delacroix's. Variants such as the charcoal in Cambridge and the pastel in Lausanne (158, 175), both made about 1900, fill the almost square sheet with the powerfully drawn pose but, once more, exact interrelationships are unclear. Each is on tracing paper and might have been taken from the other; the rubbed surface of the pastel suggests a counterproof may have been made from it, while the charcoal drawing's more resolved hips might have been an amendment of the weaker forms in the pastel. Indeed, from the lithographs onwards Degas had difficulty with the articulation of the hips and legs he had added to the Delacroix-derived pose. The statuette he made of it (176) may have been an attempt to find a solution by envisaging the standing figure in the round; elsewhere he masked the problem with drapery or furniture. He also adapted the tilting back and dangling hair to a seated pose (159, 177) in a group of powerful variants which were also explored in

177 Degas, *Seated Nude drying her Neck and Back*, c. 1900–5.
Charcoal and pastel. 121 × 101 cms.
Stuttgart, Staatsgalerie, Graphische Sammlung.

Sickert recalled that when he paid his last visit to Degas's studio, perhaps about 1910, 'he showed me a little statuette of a dancer he had on the stocks, and – it was night – he held a candle up, and turned the statuette to show me the succession of shadows cast by its silhouette on a white sheet'[196] (178). This incident is surely more than a pleasant caprice on the part of the elderly Degas. Rather, it is indicative of many of Degas's most strongly held notions about the making of art: the idea of the motif as never entirely finished, constantly in flux and the source of many variations, the commitment to the studio as a space for private thought and ceaseless experiment. These notions underpin the improvisatory and innovatory elements in Degas's creative practice – the essays in monotype or *essence*, the use of sculpture or photography in lieu of drawing, the repetition of motifs via reversal or reworking – and were revolutionary by the standards of his day. But that practice also involved factors that were insistently traditional. Degas's response to past art

was not only an active element in his late work, seen in his multiple adaptations of the pose derived from Delacroix, for instance, but also an intellectual allegiance to a canon of ideal beauty which strove to harmonize line and colour. His ambitions to produce decorative works on a grand scale, his copying of Mantegna's *Virtues Victorious over the Vices* in the Louvre as late as 1897,[197] and his career-long interest in frieze-like designs, often with the figures set in low relief, all have their roots in the training he had imbibed as a young artist.

Degas drew furthest away from that training, and his methods became most varied and experimental, during the 1870s. It is no coincidence that at that time his art was at its most public, both in the fact that it was widely exhibited and because the subjects were emphatically contemporary. With Degas's failure as a public figure – the mixed critical fortunes at the Impressionist exhibitions, the aborted projects for prints, illustrations and, in all probability, sculpture, the unfulfilled decorative ambitions – he returned to the privacy of his studio, from which he had so tentatively emerged, at the late age of thirty-one, to exhibit at the 1865 Salon. In a sense,

the two decades of the public Degas, of Degas as an exhibitor, from 1865 to 1886, were an hiatus, even an aberration, in his career. Yet, with hindsight, we can see how even at this period there were aspects of his work, such as his use of *contraposto* or reversed poses, that refer back to his earlier and look forward to his later work.

This extraordinary career increasingly appears to form a pattern of paradox and tension, between innovation and convention, the public and the private. Yet within this is unmistakable continuity, manifested above all in a belief in drawing as the fundamental vehicle of form, and in an insistence on the important lessons of past art, against which the standards of one's own art should be judged. Degas's almost self-destructive perfectionism may not have allowed the fullest flowering of his talents for which he must have dreamt. But his immense skills as draughtsman and colourist, his restless appetite for combining the most stimulating pictorial possibilities of the old and the new, and his intense frankness of vision force one to agree with Odilon Redon's judgement on Degas: 'Respect here, absolute respect.'

**178** Degas, *Grande Arabesque, second time, c.*1890–1900.
Bronze. Height: 43 cms. Private collection. CAT. 93

# Notes

The following abbreviations have been used:

L: P.-A. Lemoisne, *Degas et son oeuvre*, 4 vols, Paris, 1946–9. L. I refers to the text volume.

L.Suppl: P. Brame/T. Reff/A. Reff, *Degas et son oeuvre. A Supplement*, New York/London, 1984.

Nb: T. Reff, *The Notebooks of Edgar Degas*, 2 vols, Oxford, 1976. *Notebooks* I refers to the text in vol. I; other references are to specific notebook pages.

Vente: *Vente Atelier Degas. Catalogue des Tableaux, Pastels, et Dessins par Edgar Degas et Provenant de son Atelier*, Paris, Galerie Georges Petit, I, 6–8 May 1918; II, 11–13 December 1918; III, 7–9 April 1919; IV, 2–4 July 1919.

J: E.P. Janis, *Degas Monotypes, Essay, Catalogue and Checklist*, Cambridge, Mass., Fogg Art Museum, April–June 1968.

RS: S.W. Reed/B.S. Shapiro, *Edgar Degas: The Painter as Printmaker*, Boston, Museum of Fine Arts, November 1984–January 1985 (subsequently Philadelphia; London).

Rewald: J. Rewald, *Degas. Works in Sculpture*, London, 1944.

1 Goncourt, 1956, vol. 10, p. 164; entry of 13 February 1874.

2 Moore, 1890, p. 423.

3 *Collection Edgar Degas*, Paris, Galerie Georges Petit, 26–7 March 1918.

4 Vollard, 1924, p. 64.

5 Vollard, 1937, p. 207.

6 L. I, p. 9; Reff, *Art Bulletin* 1964, p. 555.

7 For Lamothe's teaching see Duparc, 1872, pp. 14–15, and for the practice of copying in the 19th century see Boime, 1971, esp. pp. 122–32.

8 For Degas's copying practice see Reff, 1963; *Burlington Magazine*, 1964; 1965; 1971; and *Notebooks* I, esp. pp. 13–28; Fries, 1964.

9 Nb. 4, p. 11.

10 For his Italian sojourn see *Degas e l'Italia*, 1984–5; McMullen, 1984, pp. 48–79.

11 Bénédite, March 1908, pp. 245, 247.

12 *Notebooks* I, p. 150; Mathieu, 1977, pp. 73–4.

13 For Degas's copies after Velasquez and Van Dyck see Nb. 12, pp. 67, 74 and 11, 72 respectively. For Moreau's see Bittler/Mathieu, 1983, nos 4776 (Botticelli), 4279, 4324, 4571, 4598–9 (Gozzoli); Mathieu, 1977, pp. 73, 268, n. 269 (Botticelli), n. 272 (Van Dyck), n. 274 (Velasquez).

14 Reff, 1967, p. 261 dates this copy c.1860, Henri Loyrette in *Degas e l'Italia*, 1984–5, no. 11, c.1855–6.

15 Reff, *Art Bulletin*, 1964, p. 555.

16 L. I, p. 31; letter of 30 November 1858.

17 Ibid, p. 4; see also Lafond I, 1918, pp. 20, 31.

18 Jeanniot, 1933, p. 158.

19 Durand-Gréville, 1925, p. 191; Fèvre, 1949, p. 33

20 Bénédite, January 1908, p. 52; entry of 30 August 1860.

21 Nb. 14, p. 1.

22 Bénédite, March 1908, pp. 242, 244.

23 L. I, p. 30; letter of 11 November 1858.

24 Boggs, 1962, p. 2.

25 *Degas e l'Italia*, 1984–5, no. 28.

26 Uffizi no. 426; Bittler/Mathieu, 1983, no. 4390.

27 Nb. 12, pp. 57, 74.

28 Ibid, pp. 7, 9, 52, 60, 64–5.

29 Lafenestre, 1891, p. 488.

30 Repr. Fèvre, 1949, opp. p. 64, between pp. 64–5; Ottawa, National Gallery of Canada; Cambridge, Fitzwilliam Museum.

31 Nb. 21, p. 4; Nb. 23, p. 4; see *Notebooks* I, pp. 26–7.

32 Nb. 21, p. 27.

33 Nb. 23, p. 46–7.

34 Vente III, no. 239ii.

35 *Selected works from the Andrew Gow Bequest*, 1978, no. 24.

36 J., p. xviii; see also R. Pickvance in *Edgar Degas, 1834–1917*, 1983, n.p.

37 *Degas in the Art Institute of Chicago*, 1984, p. 28.

38 I am grateful to Richard Kendall for this observation; for earlier identifications see Thomson, 1981, no. 14.

39 Reff, *Mind*, 1976, pp. 264–7; Millard, 1976, pp. 12–14.

40 Location unknown; repr. Millard, 1976, no. 119; for their collaboration see *Letters*, 1947, p. 185.

41 Waleffe, 1947, p. 12.

42 L. 868.

43 Repr. Fèvre, 1949, between pp. 32–3, Nb. 18, p. 105.

44 Mathieu, 1977, pp. 78, 269, n. 310; repr. *Degas e l'Italia*, 1984–5, p. 27.

45 RS 17–19.

46 Vente III, no. 158ii.

47 Nb. 21, p. 6v.

48 Nb. 22, p. 31; Vente III, no. 158iii.

49 Reff, *Mind*, 1976, pp. 101–10; R. Thomson, 'Notes on Degas's Sense of Humour', in Kendall, 1985, p. 10.

50 Duranty, 1876, pp. 24–30.

51 *Vanity Fair*, 1976, pp. 6–8; Harris, 1976.

52 Nb. 26, p. 4; Nb. 27, p. 28.

53 Location unknown; repr. Lafond I, p. 107.

54 Alley, 1958.

55 Laurens, 1901, p. 245.

56 Both Nb. 31 and the Edinburgh sheet, which has binding tears to the upper edge, measure 16.7 × 11.1 cms.

57 The Cleveland Museum of Art; Cambridge, Mass., Fogg Art Museum.

58 Nb. 31, p. 25.

59 Cambridge, Mass., Fogg Art Museum. For the genesis of this composition see *Degas 1879*, 1979, nos 55–60, and for the Degas–Martelli relationship Vitali, 1963, pp. 269–70.

60 Nb. 2, p. 54.

61 Rouault, 1971, p. 97.

62 Burnell, 1969; Davies, 1970, pp. 48–51; *Degas in the Art Institute of Chicago*, 1984, no. 9.

63 Found, for instance, in Jouffroy's bas-relief of *Louis-Philippe greeting the remains of Napoleon* (1851; Paris, Invalides).

64 Reff, 1963, p. 243, fig. 3; *Burlington Magazine*, 1964, p. 254, fig. 9.

65 Nb. 2, p. 68.

66 Moore, 1890, p. 421; Blanche, 1919, pp. 294–5. See also Duret, 1894, p. 204; Marx, 1897, p. 320.

67 C. Moffett, 'Disarray and Disappointment', in *The New Painting*, 1986, p. 299.

68 I shall discuss the subject-matter of *The Young Spartans* in my forthcoming *Degas: The Nudes*.

69 Havemeyer, 1961, p. 256.

70 Delacroix, 1971, p. 354; letter of 18 April 1859.

71 Guest, 1974, pp. 215–19.

72 Nb. 20, pp. 20–1.

73 L. 147, 149.

74 Lafenestre, 1891, p. 486.

75 Reff, 1963, p. 245.

76 Nb. 22, p. 133.

77 Jamot, 1924, p. 134; Halèvy, 1960, p. 24.

78 Pečírka/Pickvance, 1969, p. 23.

79 Reff, 1969, p. 284; letter of 26 April 1859.

80 Claretie, 1876, p. 270 (reprinted from review of 1874 Salon).

81 Ibid, p. 271.

82 Moore, 1890, p. 423.

83 For the primary account of Degas's early ballet pictures see Pickvance, 1963.

84 L. 299, 300, 300bis; Vente IV, nos 113b, 124; Pickvance, 1963, p. 258.

85 'Vieil Abonné', 1887, p. 26.

86 Hertz, 1920, p. 20.

87 Pickvance, 1963, p. 259.

88 For the dating of *The Rehearsal* see Roberts, 1963.

89 See n. 1 above.

90 For Degas and Mantegna see Tietze-Conrat, 1944; *Second Sight*, 1981–2.

91 For the authoritative account of the *Dance Class* see *Degas: The Dancers*, 1984–5, pp. 43–63.

92 Isaacson, 1982, pp. 98–9, 102.

93 J. Claretie, pref. to Magnier, 1885, p. iii.

94 Anon., 1926, p. 63.

95 'Vieil Abonné', 1887, p. 284; Vizentini, 1868, pp. 23–4.

96 Reff, 1981.

97 L. 512, 617, 783.

98 Mantz, 1877.

99 J. 195–200.

100 J. 212–14.

101 Bigot, 1877, p. 1027.

102 For other recent views on this aspect of Degas see C. Stuckey, 'Degas as an Artist: Revised and Still Unfinished', in *Degas: Form and Space*, 1984, pp. 13–64; *Degas: The Dancers*, 1984–5, p. 22.

103 For the genesis of this painting see *Degas 1879*, 1979, nos 2–12.

104 *Photography: the first eighty years*, 1976, no. 15.

105 Bigot, 1877, p. 1047; Rivière, 1877, p. 301; Huysmans, 1880 (1929, p. 134).

106 Goncourt, 1956, vol. 11, pp. 192–3 (entry of 14 May 1878); *La Vie Moderne*, 18 June 1881, p. 388.

107 L. I, p. 71; letter of René de Gas, 17 July 1872.

108 For Degas and the café-concert see Shapiro, 1980; D. Druick/ P. Zegers, 'Degas and the Printed Image, 1856–1914' in RS. pp.xlvii– xlix.

109 Nb. 29, pp. 11, 13, 15.

110 For this process see RS. 30.

111 See n. 15 above.

112 Nb. 3, pp. 42–5; *Notebooks* I, p. 23; Stuckey, in *Degas: Form and Space*, 1984, p. 14.

113 RS. 51–2; for *Le Jour et la Nuit* see Druick/Zegers, ibid, pp. xxxix–li.

114 *The Etruscan Sarcophagus* sheet's measurements (10.5 × 16.5 cms) suggest it came from Nb. 31; see n. 56 above.

115 Letter to Henry Lerolle, 21 August 1884; *Letters*, 1947, p. 81.

116 Sickert, 1947, p. 150.

117 Giese, 1978; Thomson in Kendall, 1985, pp. 13–14.

118 Ephrussi, 1881, p. 126.

119 For the critical reaction see Millard, 1976, pp. 119–26.

120 In 1897 he explained he had been making sculpture for thirty years: Thiébault-Sisson, 1921.

121 Rewald, p. 6; *Degas 1879*, 1979, pp. 64–7.

122 Nb. 30, pp. 29, 65, 210.

123 *Degas: The Dancers*, 1984–5, pp. 65–83.

124 See also the copies after *Hercules Bibax*, Nb. 2, p. 63; 'Bouchardon's' *Écorché*, Nb. 8, pp. 2v, 3, 32v, 37v, 43; Nb. 9, p. 18; and Gericault's *Écorché Horse*, Nb. 18, pp. 93–4.

125 See the studies of an Italian model, c.1856: The Art Institute of Chicago; Vente IV, nos 94a–c; or *Degas e l'Italia*, 1984–5, no. 31.

126 L. 504–6; L. 740, 742.

127 Nb. 34, pp. 13, 17, 19; for this sculpture see Reff, *Mind*, 1976, pp. 257–63.

128 Vollard, 1924, pp. 77–8.

129 Nb. 1, p. 12.

130 Silvestre, 1874; Burty, 1876, p. 363; Sébillot, 1877.

131 Wildenstein nos 416, 418, 420, 433; Daulte, 1971, nos 218–19; Thomson, 1984.

132 Geffroy, 1886; 1894, pp. 179–80.

133 L. 532.

134 *Degas: The Dancers*, 1984–5, pp. 79–81, 103–7; Stuckey in *Degas: Form and Space*, 1984, p. 52.

135 Nb. 7, p. 5v, a design for a lunette; Nb. 18, pp. 123, 204, a study for the décor of a library and notes on a decorative family portrait.

136 Letter of 16 October 1883; *Letters*, 1947, p. 74.

137 *Crisis of Impressionism*, 1979–80, pp. 59–60; Daulte, 1971, nos 230–3, 259; Pissarro/Venturi, 1939, no. 525.

138 See the unpublished letters from Zandomeneghi to Lucien Pissarro, 16 April 1894, 29 July 1912 (Oxford, Ashmolean Museum, Pissarro Archive).

139 Nb. 31, p. 70; for the fullest account see *Degas: The Dancers*, 1984–5, pp. 85–107.

140 Ibid, pp. 89–90.

141 RS. 59 give it to c.1891.

142 For contrasting views see Reff, 1974, p. 37; *Degas: The Dancers*, 1984–5, p. 106.

143 Lafond II, 1919, opp. p. 30, reproduces these as a pair, while regretting (I, 1918, p. 38) that Degas never executed a decorative work.

144 L. 473 was first owned by Robert de Bonnières, L. 486 by Henry Lerolle.

145 L. 523.

146 Johnston, 1982, no. 41.

147 Delaunay's is in the Église de la Trinité, Paris (1867), Bonnat's is in St André, Bayonne.

148 See Thomson in Kendall, 1985, p. 15.

149 See n. 129 above.

150 Lafond I, 1918, pp. 38–9.

151 Letter of 9 September 1882; *Letters*, 1947, p. 71.

152 Letter of 1 January 1859, L. I, pp. 31–2.

153 Duranty, 1876, p. 25.

154 Letter of de Gas père, 21 November 1863; letter of René de Gas, 22 April 1864; L. I, p. 41.

155 Letter of 21 August 1884; *Letters*, 1947, p. 81; see also 9 September 1882, 16 August 1884, ibid, pp. 71, 80–1.

156 Lafond I, 1918, p. 28.

157 For the best account of these pictures see *Degas's Racing World*, 1968.

158 Reff, *Burlington Magazine*, 1964, p. 258; Nb. 2, pp. 43, 55, 62, 66; Nb. 3, pp. 41, 39–6, 28, 19, 17.

159 Cambridge, Mass., Fogg Art Museum; Amsterdam, Rijksmuseum; Bittler/Mathieu, 1983, nos 4279, 4324.

160 Nb. 14, p. 79; Nb. 16, p. 38; Nb. 19, p. 42.

161 The others are L. 75–6.

162 L. I, p. 40; he produced a pastel of the same motif c.1890, L. 850.

163 Nb. 20, pp. 29, 31; Nb. 22, pp. 123, 127; Nb. 23, p. 41.

164 *Notebooks* I, p. 21 and n. 7; L. 502–3, 761.

165 For destroying sculpture see Vollard, 1924, pp. 112–13.

166 L. 762, c.1885–90.

167 Vente III, no. 89; Vente IV, nos 208d, 218b, 391.

168 Nb. 29, p. 81.

169 L. 665, 665bis.

170 Vente IV, no. 335b.

171 Letter of 27 November 1872; *Letters*, 1947, p. 21.

172 L. 960–1; L. 1419–20, 1420bis.

173 For instance L. 682, 693, 781.

174 Nb. 30, p. 208.

175 Rouart. 1945, p. 63; Reff, *Mind*, 1976, p. 282; *Degas: The Dancers*, 1984–5, p. 123.

176 Maison, 1956, p. 162.

177 For example Nb. 8, p. 53; Pickvance, 1963, p. 264.

178 L. 1277, 1281; Vente II, no. 277; Vente III, nos 207i, 300–1.

179 Lafond I, 1918, p. 20.

180 For the authoritative account see *Degas: The Dancers*, 1984–5, pp. 109–27.

181 L. 1274, 1344, 1352.

182 Lemoisne was well aware of this when he compiled his catalogue raisonné; see under L. 515.

183 H. Adhémar, 1967, p. 297.

184 *Degas: The Dancers*, 1984–5, p. 112; Buerger, 1978, p. 20. Degas had exhibited photographs with his work as early as 1876 (Pickvance, 1963, p. 265), but probably did not begin to take them himself until c.1889 (E.P. Janis, 'Edgar Degas's Photographic Theatre', in *Degas: Form and Space*, 1984, p. 465).

185 L. 1271bis.

186 L. 1352.

187 Letter of 17 January 1886; *Letters*, 1947, p. 119.

188 Letter of 6 December 1891; ibid, p. 175.

189 Halévy, 1960, p. 67.

190 Reff, *Burlington Magazine*, 1964, p. 252; *Mind*, 1976, pp. 58–9.

191 Chappuis, 1973, no. 673 (c.1883–6).

192 For these prints see RS, pp. lxii–lxx, nos 61–6.

193 RS 66.

194 Rewald, nos LXX–LXXII, LXIX.

195 Letter of 22 April 1864; L. I, p. 41.

196 Sickert, 1947, p. 148.

197 Reff, *Mind*, 1976, pp. 296–8.

# Bibliography

The following bibliography is not intended as a comprehensive survey of the multitudinous publications on Degas. Rather it is a list of the writings I have found most useful in the preparation of *The Private Degas*, with an emphasis on the recent literature.

The titles most frequently referred to are listed as abbreviations at the beginning of the Notes, p. 132.

H. ADHÉMAR, 'Edgar Degas et la "Scène de Guerre au Moyen-Age"', *Gazette des Beaux-Arts*, 70, November 1967, pp. 295–8.

J. ADHÉMAR/F. CACHIN, *Degas: The Complete Etchings, Lithographs and Monotypes*, London, 1974.

R. ALLEY, 'Notes on some works by Degas, Utrillo and Chagall in the Tate Gallery', *Burlington Magazine*, C, May 1958, p. 171.

ANON., *More Uncensored Recollections*, London, 1926.

L. BÉNÉDITE, 'Artistes Contemporains. J.-J. Henner', *Gazette des Beaux-Arts*, 35, January 1906, pp. 39–48; 36, November 1906, pp. 393–406; 38, October 1907, pp. 315–32; November 1907, pp. 408–23; 39, January 1908, pp. 35–58; March 1908, pp. 237–64; 40, August 1908, pp. 137–66.

C. BIGOT, 'L'Exposition des "Impressionnistes"', *Revue politique et littéraire*, 28 April 1877, pp. 1045–8.

P. BITTLER/P.-L. MATHIEU, *Musée Gustave Moreau, Catalogue des dessins de Gustave Moreau*, Paris, 1983.

J.-E. BLANCHE, *Propos de Peintre. De David à Degas*, Paris, 1919.

J.S. BOGGS, *Portraits by Degas*, Berkeley/Los Angeles, 1962.

J.S. BOGGS, '"Danseuses à la barre" by Degas', *Bulletin of the National Gallery of Canada*, 2, 1964, pp. 1–9.

A. BOIME, *The Academy and French painting in the Nineteenth Century*, London, 1971.

L. BROWSE, *Degas Dancers*, London, 1949.

J. BUERGER, 'Degas' Solarized and Negative Photographs: A Look at Unorthodox Classicism', *Image*, 21, June 1978, pp. 17–23.

D. BURNELL, 'Degas and his "Young Spartans Exercising"', *Art Institute of Chicago Museum Studies*, IV, 1969, pp. 49–65.

P. BURTY, 'The Exhibition of the "Intransigeants"', *The Academy*, 15 April 1876, pp. 363–4.

A. CHAPPUIS, *The Drawings of Paul Cézanne. A Catalogue Raisonné*, 2 vols, London, 1973.

J. CLARETIE, *L'Art et les Artistes français contemporains*, Paris, 1876.

*The Crisis of Impressionism, 1878–1882*, Ann Arbor, University of Michigan Museum of Art, November 1979–January 1980.

F. DAULTE, *Auguste Renoir, catalogue raisonné de l'oeuvre peint, I, Figures, 1860–1890*, Lausanne, 1971.

M. DAVIES, *National Gallery Catalogues, French School*, revised ed., London, 1970.

*Degas, Letters*, ed. M. Guérin, Oxford, 1947 [cited as *Letters*]. French edition, *Lettres de Degas*, Paris, 1945.

*Degas's Racing World*, New York, Wildenstein, March–April 1968.

*Degas: Pastels and Drawings*, Nottingham University Art Gallery, January–February 1969.

*Degas: Oeuvres du Musée du Louvre, Peintures, Pastels, Dessins, Sculptures*, Paris, Orangerie des Tuileries, June–September 1969.

*Edgar Degas: The Reluctant Impressionist*, Boston, Museum of Fine Arts, June–September 1974.

*Edgar Degas*, New York, Acquavella Galleries, November–December 1978.

*Degas and the Dance*, Northampton, Mass., Smith College Museum of Art, April–May 1979.

*Degas 1879*, Edinburgh, National Gallery of Scotland, August–September 1979.

*Edgar Degas, 1834–1917*, London, David Carritt Ltd, November–December 1983.

*Degas: Pastelle, Ölskizzen, Zeichnungen*, Tübingen/Berlin, 1984.

*Degas: Form and Space*, Paris, Centre Culturel du Marais, 1984.

*Degas in the Art Institute of Chicago*, Chicago, Art Institute, July–September 1984.

*Degas: The Dancers*, Washington, National Gallery of Art, November 1984–March 1985.

*Degas e l'Italia*, Rome, Villa Medici, December 1984–February 1985.

*Von Delacroix bis Maillol*, Bremen, Kunsthalle, March–April 1969.

E. DELACROIX, *Selected Letters*, ed. J. Stewart, London, 1971.

*Drawings by Degas*, Philadelphia/Minneapolis/St Louis, 1967.

*Drawings from the David Daniels Collection*, Minneapolis/Chicago/Kansas City/Cambridge, Mass., 1968.

I. DUNLOP, *Degas*, New York, 1979.

A. DUPARC (ed.), *Correspondance de Henri Regnault*, Paris, 1872.

E. DURAND-GRÉVILLE, *Entretiens de J.-J. Henner*, Paris, 1925.

E. DURANTY, *La Nouvelle Peinture*, Paris, 1976.

T. DURET, 'Degas', *Art Journal*, 1894, pp. 204–8.

C. E(PHRUSSI), 'Exposition des artistes indépendants', *La Chronique des arts et de la curiosité*, 16 April 1881, pp. 126–7.

J. FÈVRE, *Mon oncle Degas*, Geneva, 1949.

G. FRIES, 'Degas et les maîtres', *Art de France*, IV, 1964, pp. 352–9.

G. GEFFROY, 'Hors du Salon. Les Impressionnistes', *La Justice*, 26 May 1886.

G. GEFFROY, *La Vie Artistique, Histoire de l'Impressionnisme*, Paris, 1894.

M. GERSTEIN, 'Degas's Fans', *Art Bulletin*, 64, March 1982, pp. 105–18.

L. GIESE, 'A Visit to the Museum', *Bulletin of the Museum of Fine Arts, Boston*, 76, 1978, pp. 42–53.

E. DE GONCOURT, 'Notes d'un Parisien', *La Vie Moderne*, 25, 18 June 1881, p. 388.

E. & J. DE GONCOURT, *Journal. Mémoires de la vie littéraire*, ed. R. Ricatte, 22 vols, Monaco, 1956.

I. GUEST, *The Ballet of the Second Empire*, London, 1974.

I. GUEST, *Jules Perrot, Master of the Romantic Ballet*, London, 1984.

D. HALÉVY, *Degas parle*, Paris, 1960.

L. HALÉVY, *La Famille Cardinal*, Paris, 1883.

E. HARRIS, 'Carlo Pellegrini: Man and "Ape"', *Apollo*, CIII, January 1976, pp. 53–7.

L. HAVEMEYER, *Sixteen to Sixty, Memoirs of a Collector*, New York, 1961.

E. HAVERCAMP-BEGEMANN ET AL., *Drawings from the Clark Institute: The Catalogue Raisonné*, 2 vols, New Haven/London, 1964.

H. HERTZ, *Degas*, Paris, 1920.

H.R. HOETINK, *Franse Tekeningen uit de 19e eeuw*, Rotterdam, Boymans-van Beuningen Museum, 1968.

J.-K. HUYSMANS, 'L'Exposition des Indépendants en 1880' (*Oeuvres complètes de J.-K. Huysmans, VI, L'Art Moderne*, Paris, 1929, pp. 130–9).

J. ISAACSON, 'Impressionism and Journalistic Illustration', *Arts Magazine*, 56, June 1982, pp. 95–115.

P. JAMOT, *Degas*, Paris, 1924.

G. JEANNIOT, 'Souvenirs sur Degas', *Revue Universelle*, LV, 1933, pp. 152–74, 280–304.

W.R. JOHNSTON, *The Nineteenth Century Paintings in the Walters Art Gallery*, Baltimore, 1982.

R. KENDALL (ed.), *Degas, 1834–1917*, Manchester, 1985.

R.W. KENNEDY, 'Degas and Raphael', *Smith College Museum of Art Bulletin*, 33–4, 1953, pp. 5–12.

G. LAFENESTRE, 'Elie Delaunay', *Gazette des Beaux-Arts*, 6, November 1891, pp. 353–65; December 1891, pp. 484–500.

P. LAFOND, *Degas*, 2 vols, Paris, 1918–19.

J. LAURENS, *La Légende des Ateliers: fragments et notes d'un artiste-peintre, de 1842 à 1900*, Carpentras, 1901.

M. MAGNIER, *La Danseuse*, Paris, 1885.

K.E. MAISON, 'Further Daumier Studies, I: The Tracings', *Burlington Magazine*, XCVIII, May 1956, pp.162–6.

P. MANTZ, 'L'Exposition des Peintres Impressionnistes', *Le Temps*, 22 April 1877, p. 2.

R. MARX, 'Cartons d'artistes. Degas', *L'Image*, 11, October 1897, pp. 320–5.

P.-L. MATHIEU, *Gustave Moreau*, Oxford, 1977.

R. McMULLEN, *Degas, His Life, Times and Work*, Boston, 1984.

C. MILLARD, *The Sculpture of Edgar Degas*, Princeton, 1976.

G. MOORE, 'Degas: The Painter of Modern Life', *Magazine of Art*, 13, 1890, pp. 416–25.

*The New Painting: Impressionism, 1874–1886*, Washington/San Francisco, 1986.

J. PÉCÍRKA/R. PICKVANCE, *Degas, Drawings*, London, 1969.

*Photography: the first eighty years*, London, Colnaghi, October–December 1976.

R. PICKVANCE, 'Degas's Dancers: 1872–6', *Burlington Magazine*, CV, June 1963, pp. 256–66.

L.-R. PISSARRO/L. VENTURI, *Camille Pissarro, son art, son oeuvre*, 2 vols, Paris, 1939.

P. POOL, 'Degas and Moreau', *Burlington Magazine*, CV, June 1963, pp. 251–6.

T. REFF, 'Degas's Copies of Older Art', *Burlington Magazine*, CV, June 1963, pp. 241–51.

T. REFF, 'New Light on Degas's Copies', *Burlington Magazine*, CVI, June 1964, pp. 250–9.

T. REFF, 'Copyists in the Louvre, 1850–1870', *Art Bulletin*, XLVI, December 1964, pp. 552–9.

T. REFF, 'Addenda on Degas's Copies', *Burlington Magazine*, CVII, June 1965, pp. 320–3.

T. REFF, 'An Exhibition of Drawings by Degas', *Art Quarterly*, XXX, 1967, pp. 253–63.

T. REFF, 'Some Unpublished Letters of Degas', *Art Bulletin*, L, March 1968, pp. 87–94.

T. REFF, 'More Unpublished Letters of Degas', *Art Bulletin*, LI, September 1969, pp. 281–9.

T. REFF, 'Further Thoughts on Degas's Copies', *Burlington Magazine*, CXIII, September 1971, pp. 534–41.

T. REFF, 'Works by Degas in the Detroit Institute of Arts', *Bulletin of the Detroit Institute of Arts*, 53, 1974, pp. 1–44.

T. REFF, *Degas: The Artist's Mind*, London, 1976. [Cited as *Mind*.]

T. REFF, 'Degas: A Master among Masters', *Metropolitan Museum Bulletin*, XXXIV, Spring 1977, pp. 1–49.

T. REFF, 'Degas and de Valernes in 1872', *Arts Magazine*, 56, September 1981, pp. 126–7.

G. RIVIÈRE, 'Les Intransigéants et les Impressionnistes. Souvenirs du Salon Libre de 1877', *L'Artiste*, II, November 1877, pp. 298–302.

G. RIVIÈRE, *M. Degas, bourgeois de Paris*, Paris, 1935.

K. ROBERTS, 'The Date of Degas's "The Rehearsal" in Glasgow', *Burlington Magazine*, CV, June 1963, pp. 280–1.

L. ROLIN, 'La "Danseuse de Quatorze Ans" de Degas, son tutu, et sa perruque', *Gazette des Beaux-Arts*, 104, November 1984, pp. 173–4.

D. ROUART, *Degas à la Recherche de sa Technique*, Paris, 1945.

G. ROUAULT, *Sur l'Art et sur la Vie*, Paris, 1971.

P. SÉBILLOT, 'Exposition des Impressionnistes', *Le Bien Public*, 7 April 1877, p. 2.

M. SHAPIRO, 'Degas and the Siamese Twins of the Café-Concert: The Ambassadeurs and the Alcazar d'Eté', *Gazette des Beaux-Arts*, 95, April 1980, pp. 153–64.

A. SCHARF, *Art and Photography*, London, 1968.

*Second Sight: Mantegna, 'Samson and Delilah'; Degas, 'Beach Scene'*, London, National Gallery, November 1981–January 1982.

*Selected works from the Andrew Gow Bequest*, London, Hazlitt, Gooden and Fox, October–November 1978.

W. SICKERT, *A Free House!*, ed. O. Sitwell, London, 1947.

A. SILVESTRE, 'Physiologie du Refusé. L'Exposition des Révoltés', *L'Opinion nationale*, 22 April 1874, p. 2.

G. SZABO, *Nineteenth Century French Drawings from the Robert Lehman Collection*, New York, Metropolitan Museum, 1980.

A. TERRASSE, *Degas et la photographie*, Paris, 1983.

F. THIÉBAULT-SISSON, 'Degas Sculpteur', *Le Temps*, 23 May 1921, p. 3.

R. THOMSON, 'Degas in Edinburgh', *Burlington Magazine*, CXXI, October 1979, pp. 674–7.

R. THOMSON, *French Nineteenth Century Drawings in the Whitworth Art Gallery*, Manchester, 1981.

R. THOMSON, 'Degas's "Torse de Femme" and Titian', *Gazette des Beaux-Arts*, 98, July–August 1981, pp. 45–8.

R. THOMSON, 'Manet's "Les Vins de France"', *Gazette des Beaux-Arts*, 104, October 1984, p. 138.

E. TIETZE-CONRAT, 'What Degas learnt from Mantegna', *Gazette des Beaux-Arts*, 24, July 1944, pp. 413–20.

P. VALÉRY, *Degas, danse, dessin*, Paris, 1938.

*Vanity Fair: an exhibition of original cartoons*, London, National Portrait Gallery, July–August 1976.

K. VARNEDOE, 'On Degas's Sculpture', *Arts Magazine*, 52, November 1977, pp. 116–19.

K. VARNEDOE, 'The Ideology of Time: Degas and Photography', *Art in America*, 68, Summer 1980, pp. 96–110.

'Un Vieil Abonné', *Ces Demoiselles de l'Opéra*, Paris, 1887.

L. VITALI, 'Three Italian Friends of Degas', *Burlington Magazine*, CV, June 1963, pp. 266–73.

A. VIZENTINI, *Derrière la Toile, Foyers, Coulisses et Comédiens*, Paris, 1868.

A. VOLLARD, *Degas*, Paris, 1924.

A. VOLLARD, *Souvenirs d'un marchand de tableaux*, Paris, 1937.

M. DE WALEFFE, *Quand Paris était un paradis*, Paris, 1947.

J. WALKER, 'Degas et les maîtres anciens', *Gazette des Beaux-Arts*, 6, September 1933, pp. 173–85.

D. WILDENSTEIN, *Claude Monet. Biographie et catalogue raisonné*, I, Lausanne/Paris, 1974.

# Chronology

**1834** Born 19 July, in Paris. Son of Auguste de Gas (1807–74) and his wife Marie Célestine (*née* Musson; 1815–47); they had married in 1832. Four other children followed: Achille (1838–93), Thérèse (1840–97), Marguerite (1842–95) and René (1845–1926).

**1845–53** Attended Lycée Louis-le-Grand, Paris. Taught drawing by Léon Cogniet. Awarded *baccalauréat*, 23 March 1853.

**1853** As pupil of Félix Barrias, registered as copyist at the Louvre on 7 April and at the Bibliothèque Impériale (Bibliothèque Nationale) on 9 April.

**1855** 6 April: enrolled at the Ecole des Beaux-Arts, as a pupil of Louis Lamothe.
Met and advised by Ingres, whose work he studied at the Universal Exhibition.
July–September: tour of Rhone valley, including Lyons, Arles and Avignon, as well as Sète and Montpellier.

**1856** October–July 1857: studied in Rome, sitting in on life classes at the official French School, the Villa Medici, under the directorship of Victor Schnetz. Established close contacts with Gustave Moreau, Elie Delaunay, Léon Bonnat, etc.

**1857** July–October: studied in Naples; visited family there.
November–July 1858: studied in Rome.

**1858** July: travelled via Viterbo, Orvieto, Perugia, Assisi and Arezzo to Florence.
August–March 1859: studied in Florence, Sienna. Close to Moreau.

**1859** February–March: visited Pisa, Sienna. April: travelled via Pisa, Genoa, Turin to Paris. Much impressed by Delacroix at the Salon.

**1860** March–April: revisited Florence, Naples.

**1861** September–October: visited stud of school-friend Paul Valpinçon, Ménil-Hubert, Normandy.

**1860s** There is little information about this period. Contrary to what is usually believed, he continued his artistic rather than merely social contacts with his academic friends well into the second half of the decade – advising Henner on his Salon picture of 1868 – and befriended independents such as Manet, Whistler and Fantin-Latour at the beginning of the 1860s. Degas no doubt paid occasional visits to his family in Italy, and probably visited London.

**1865** Exhibited at the Salon: *Medieval War Scene* (L.124; Paris, Musée d'Orsay).

**1866** Exhibited at the Salon: *Steeplechase Scene* (L.140; Upperville, Virginia, Mellon Collection).

**1867** Exhibited at the Salon: *Family Portrait* (? L.79; *The Bellelli Family*, Paris, Musée d'Orsay) and *Family Portrait* (? L.131 or L.164; *Edmondo and Thérèse Morbilli*, Washington, National Gallery/Boston, Museum of Fine Arts).

**1868** 26 March: fifth re-registration to copy at the Louvre, sponsored by Emile Lévy.
Exhibited at the Salon: *Portrait of Mlle E.F. . . . à propos the ballet 'La Source'* (L.146; New York, Brooklyn Museum; 46).

**1869** February: visited Brussels to negotiate a business arrangement with dealer Arthur Stevens. Refused contract worth 12,000 francs per annum.
Exhibited at the Salon: *Portrait of Mme G . . .* (L.165; *Josephine Gaujelin*, Boston, Mass., Isabella Stewart Gardner Museum). *Mme Camus at the Piano* (L.207; Zurich, Bührle Collection) refused by Salon Jury.

**1870** 12 April: open letter to Salon Jury in *Paris-Journal* with proposals for a new system of hanging.
Exhibited at the Salon: *Portrait of Mme C . . .* (L.271; *Mme Camus*, Washington, National Gallery of Art) and *Portrait of Mme G . . .* (L.214; *Mme Yves Gobillard*, New York, Metropolitan Museum).

**1870–1** Franco–Prussian War. During the

Siege of Paris (September 1870–January 1871) served in the artillery under his schoolfriend Henri Rouart. From this time he began to suffer problems with his eyesight.

**1871** March–May: during the Commune retreated to Ménil-Hubert.
October: visited London.

**1872** October to March 1873: travelled to New Orleans with René.

**1873** December: visited Turin to nurse ailing father.

**1874** 23 February: death of Auguste de Gas. For at least the remainder of the decade Degas's financial position was very weak, having repaid René's debts to the family bank.
April–May: first Impressionist exhibition; 10 works in catalogue.

**1875** March–April: visited Naples, Florence, Pisa, Genoa.
September: may have visited London.

**1876** April: second Impressionist exhibition; 24 works in catalogue.
June–July: visited Naples.

**1877** April–May: third Impressionist exhibition; 25 works in catalogue, probably including *Café-concert des Ambassadeurs* (100) and *Two Dancers at the Bar* (61).
September: stayed at Ménil-Hubert.

**1878** *Portraits in a Cotton Office, New Orleans* (1873; L. 320) purchased by the Musée des Beaux-Arts, Pau, on the advice of Paul Lafond; it was Degas's first painting to enter a public collection.

**1879** April–May: fourth Impressionist exhibition; 25 works in catalogue, including five fans, *Diego Martelli* (30), *Miss Lala at the Circus Fernando* (119), and *Laundresses carrying their Linen in Town* (134). Degas introduced friends such as Mary Cassatt, Jean-Louis Forain and Federigo Zandomeneghi. Collaboration on *Le Jour et la Nuit* with Cassatt, Camille Pissarro, Félix Bracquemond, etc.

**1880** April: fifth Impressionist exhibition; 8 paintings and pastels in catalogue, including *The Young Spartans Exercising* (37), which was probably not shown, several drawings

and etchings, among them *Mary Cassatt at the Louvre* (104). The *Little Dancer of Fourteen Years* was catalogued but not exhibited.

**1881** April–May: sixth Impressionist exhibition: 7 pictures in catalogue, as well as the *Little Dancer of Fourteen Years* (110).

**1882** Did not submit work to seventh Impressionist exhibition.
July: stayed at Etretat with the Halévys.
September: visited Geneva.

**1884** August–October: stayed at Ménil-Hubert, working on bust of Paul Valpinçon's. daughter, Hortense.

**1885** Summer: at Dieppe with Halévys, Jacques-Emile Blanche, Henri Gervex, Walter Sickert, Paul Gauguin. Commissioned work from photographer Barnes.
August: visited St Malo, Mont St Michel.

**1886** January: visited Naples.
May–June: eighth Impressionist exhibition; 15 works in catalogue. About this time Degas ceased to use notebooks.

**1888** December: declined invitation to exhibit in Brussels with Les XX.

**1889** Refused to participate in the Universal Exhibition.
September: with Giovanni Boldini travelled to Spain, visiting the Prado, and to Morocco.

**1890** Moved to accommodation in the rue Victor-Massé. It was from this period that Degas began to experiment with photography and started to build up his collection, by purchase and exchange, which came to include, alongside some old master paintings, major works by Ingres, Delacroix, Corot, Daumier, Gavarni, Manet, Pissarro, Cézanne, Gauguin and Van Gogh. He continued to encourage young artists, including Suzanne Valadon, Charles Maurin, Henri de Toulouse-Lautrec, Rupert Carabin, and William Rothenstein.
September–October: travelled with Paul-Albert Bartholomé from Paris to Diénay (Burgundy) in a carriage pulled by a white horse (which Degas painted with black stripes to amaze passers-by).

**1892** October: landscape monotypes exhibited at Durand-Ruel Gallery, Paris.

**1897** Copied Mantegna's *Virtues Victorious over the Vices* in the Louvre, with Ernest Rouart.
Visited Montauban with Bartholomé to study Ingres's drawings.
Broke with the Halévys over the Dreyfus Affair. Extreme anti-semitism.

**1900** Work exhibited at the Universal Exhibition against his will.

**1903** Three waxes cast in plaster.

**1904** *Half-length Dancer* (151) entered Kunsthalle, Bremen.

**1911** Visited Ingres exhibition at the Galerie Georges Petit; could scarcely see exhibits.

**1912** Works by Degas fetched huge prices at the sale of Henri Rouart's collection.
Forced to move from rue Victor-Massé; probably ceased to produce work.

**1917** 27 September: died. Funeral at Saint-Jean-l'Evangeliste, Paris, attended by Cassatt, Forain, Gervex, Bonnat, Batholomé, Zandomeneghi, Joseph and Georges Durand-Ruel, Claude Monet, etc.

# Catalogue

Works are listed in chronological order; all are on white paper, unless otherwise stated. Measurements are given in centimetres, height before width. 'Lugt' refers to F. Lugt, *Les marques de Collections de Dessins et d'Estampes*, Amsterdam, 1921 (only the two Degas stamps have been cited). Reference is provided to the Degas Vente catalogues or the standard catalogue raisonné where appropriate; for these, see Bibliography.

1 Copy after Raphael, *School of Athens*, c.1853.
Pencil.
23 × 15 cms.
Stamp l.r: Lugt 657.
The Visitors of the Ashmolean Museum, Oxford.

2 Copy after the Parthenon Frieze, c.1853–4.
Pencil on grey paper.
23.5 × 30.2 cms.
Stamp verso: Lugt 657.
Bremen, Kunsthalle.

3 Copy after Mantegna, *Calvary: Crucified Thief*, c.1853–4.
Pencil, heightened with red chalk.
31 × 13.5 cms.
Stamp l.r: Lugt 658.
Vente IV, no. 99c.
Zurich, Marianne Feilchenfeldt.

4 Copy after Mantegna, *Calvary: Roman Soldier*, c.1853–5.
Pencil and black chalk.
30.8 × 21.6 cms.
Stamp l.r: Lugt 658. Verso: Lugt 657.

138

Vente IV, no. 109a.
Williamstown, Mass., Sterling and Francine Clark Art Institute.

5 Copy after Michelangelo, *Last Judgement*, c.1854–6.
Pencil.
31.5 × 23.1 cms.
Stamp verso: Lugt 657.
Bremen, Kunsthalle.

6 Copy after *The Borghese Gladiator*, c.1854–6.
Black and red chalk on grey paper.
Verso: studies after Hellenistic sculpture (black chalk).
31.1 × 24.1 cms.
Stamp: Lugt 657.
Williamstown, Mass., Sterling and Francine Clark Art Institute.

7 *Ordination Ceremony in the Cathedral at Lyons*, 1855.
Oil on paper, mounted on canvas.
31.4 × 23.3 cms.
Stamp l.r: Lugt 657.
L.Suppl. 7.
The Syndics of the Fitzwilliam Museum, Cambridge.

8 *Thérèse de Gas*, c.1855–6.
Pencil on pink paper.
Verso: study of a draped figure and a detail of drapery (black chalk, heightened with white).
Inscr: '*Les plis de la robe/sont très fixés*' '*manteau*' (?).
28.5 × 23.6 cms.
Stamp: Lugt 657.
The Syndics of the Fitzwilliam Museum, Cambridge.

9 *Self-portrait*, 1857.
Etching and drypoint.
23 × 14.4 cms (platemark).
RS. 8/iii.
Williamstown, Mass., Sterling and Francine Clark Art Institute.

10 *Sheet of Studies*, 1858–9.
Pencil, pen and ink, with green, brown and pale blue washes.

30.5 × 23.5 cms.
Inscr. l.l: 'Flor 1857'.
Stamp l.l: Lugt 658. Verso: Lugt 657.
Vente IV, no. 74b.
The Cleveland Museum of Art, John L. Severance Fund.

11 Copy after Botticelli, *The Birth of Venus*, 1859.
Pencil.
29 × 21 cms.
Stamp l.l: Lugt 658.
Vente IV, no. 99b.
Zurich, Marianne Feilchenfeldt.

12 Copy after Benozzo Gozzoli, *Journey of the Magi*, 1859 or 1860.
Pencil.
26.2 × 30.5 cms.
Inscr. u.l: 'Florence 1860' (latter number prob. inscr. over '1859').
Stamp l.r: Lugt 658.
Vente IV, no. 91c.
Cambridge, Mass., Fogg Art Museum.

13 Copy after Delacroix, *Entry of the Crusaders into Constantinople*, c.1859–60.
Oil on paper, mounted on canvas.
35 × 38 cms.
L.Suppl. 35.
On loan to Kunsthaus, Zurich.

14 Copy after Michelangelo, *Dying Slave*, c.1859–60.
Pencil.
33 × 23 cms.
Stamp l.l: Lugt 658.
Vente IV, no. 99a.
Zurich, Marianne Feilchenfeldt.

15 *Portrait of Gustave Moreau*, c.1860.
Oil on canvas.
40 × 22 cms.
L.178.
Paris, Musée Gustave Moreau.

16 *At the Races*, c.1860.
Pencil on reddish-beige paper (six pieces joined), laid down.

34.9 × 48.3 cms.
Stamp l.l: Lugt 658. Verso: Lugt 657.
Vente IV, no. 253.
Williamstown, Mass., Sterling and Francine Clark Art Institute.

17 Study for *The Young Spartans Exercising*, c.1860.
Pencil.
28.5 × 17.7 cms.
Stamp l.l: Lugt 658.
Vente I, no. 62b(?).
Detroit Institute of Arts.

18 Study for *The Young Spartans: Youth with Arms Upraised*, c.1860–1.
Pencil and black chalk.
31.7 × 19.4 cms.
Stamp l.l: Lugt 658. Verso: Lugt 657.
Vente I, no. 62b(?).
New York, The Metropolitan Museum of Art, Robert Lehman Collection, 1975.

19 Study for *The Young Spartans: Youth in an attitude of defence*, c.1860–1.
Pencil and black chalk.
43.3 × 21.3 cms.
Stamp l.l: Lugt 658. Verso: Lugt 657.
Vente I, no. 62b(?).
New York, The Metropolitan Museum of Art, Robert Lehman Collection, 1975.

20 Study for *The Young Spartans*, c.1860–1.
Oil on paper mounted on board.
21 × 28 cms.
Stamp l.l: Lugt 658.
L. 72.
Cambridge, Mass., Fogg Art Museum. Purchase, Friends of the Fogg, Hyatt Prichard and Burr Funds.

21 Study for *The Young Spartans: Kneeling Youth*, c.1860–1.
Pencil and black chalk.

22.8 × 35.2 cms.
Stamp l.l: Lugt 658.
Vente I, no. 62b(?).
Toledo Museum of Art.

**22** Study for *The Young Spartans: Standing Girl*, c. 1860–1.
Pencil.
36.9 × 23.3 cms.
Stamp l.l: Lugt 658.
Vente I, no. 62b(?).
Private collection.

**23** Study for *Edmondo and Thérèse Morbilli*, c. 1863–4.
Oil on canvas.
37 × 29 cms.
Signed l.r: 'Degas'.
L. 132.
Zurich, private collection.

**24** *Manet Seated, turned to the right*, c. 1864–5.
Etching and drypoint.
19.5 × 13 cms (platemark).
Stamp verso: Lugt 657.
RS. 18/iii.
The Art Institute of Chicago.

**25** Study for *Medieval War Scene: Standing Female Nude*, c. 1865.
Black chalk and stump.
39.3 × 22.5 cms (including additional strip to lower edge).
Stamp l.r: Lugt 658. Verso: Lugt 657.
Vente I, with no. 13.
Paris, Musée du Louvre, Département des Arts Graphiques.

**26** *Study of a Horse*, c. 1865–8.
Pencil on light grey paper.
23.7 × 26.3 cms.
Stamp l.r: Lugt 658.
Vente IV, no. 228a.
Rotterdam, Boymans-van Beuningen Museum.

**27** *Horse Drinking*, c. 1865–8.
Bronze.
Height: 16 cms.
Stamp on base: Lugt 658.
Rewald II.
Private collection.

**28** Copy after Veronese, *The Finding of Moses*, c. 1865–8.
Oil on canvas.
31.2 × 17.3 cms.
L. Suppl. 46.
The Syndics of the Fitzwilliam Museum, Cambridge.

**29** Copy after Moro, *Elisabeth of Valois*, c. 1865–70.
Black chalk, charcoal, and stump.
40.5 × 27.4 cms.
The Syndics of the Fitzwilliam Museum, Cambridge.

**30** Study for *Victoria Dubourg*, c. 1866.
Pencil and black chalk.
31.1 × 22.2 cms.
Stamp l.l: Lugt 658.
Vente II, no. 238ii.
The Cleveland Museum of Art, Mr and Mrs Lewis B. Williams Collection.

**31** Study for *James Tissot*, c. 1866–8.
Black chalk and pencil on light brown paper.
31 × 35 cms.
Stamp l.l: Lugt 658.
Vente III, no. 158a.
Cambridge, Mass., Fogg Art Museum.

**32** Study for *Mlle Fiocre: Eugénie Fiocre*, c. 1866–8.
Pencil on pink paper, laid down.
45.1 × 28 cms.
Stamp l.l: Lugt 658. Verso: Lugt 657.
Vente IV, no. 107b.
Mr David Daniels.

**33** Study for *Mlle Fiocre: Young Woman playing a Mandolin*, c. 1866–8.
Pencil.
35.5 × 21.4 cms.
Stamp l.r: Lugt 658.
Vente IV, no. 79a.
The Art Institute of Chicago, Gift of Robert Allerton.

**34** *Woman looking through Field-glasses*, c. 1866–8.

*Essence* and black chalk on paper, laid down on canvas.
31.4 × 19 cms (paper).
Inscr. on verso: 'Degas vers 1865'.
L. 268.
The Burrell Collection, Glasgow Museums and Art Galleries.

**35** *Standing Female Figure with Bared Torso*, c. 1866–8.
*Essence* on brown prepared paper.
47 × 30 cms.
Stamp l.r: Lugt 658.
L. 351.
Basel, Kunstmuseum, Öffentliche Kunstsammlungen.

**36** Copy after Mantegna, *Calvary*, c. 1868–9.
Oil on canvas.
69 × 92.5 cms.
Stamp l.r: Lugt 658.
L. 194.
Tours, Musée des Beaux-Arts.

**37** Copy after Le Sueur, *St Paul Preaching at Ephesus*, c. 1868–9.
Oil on canvas.
41.3 × 33.3 cms.
L. Suppl. 47.
Kasmin Ltd.

**38** *The Duet (The Singing Rehearsal)*, c. 1868–70.
Oil on canvas.
81 × 65 cms.
Stamp on stretcher: Lugt 657.
L. 331.
Washington, Dumbarton Oaks Research Library and Collection.

**39** Study for *The Duet*, c. 1868–70.
Pencil on beige paper.
49 × 31.2 cms.
Stamp l.l: Lugt 658. Verso: Lugt 657.
Vente III, no. 404ii.
Paris, Musée du Louvre, Département des Arts Graphiques.

**40** Study for *The Dance Rehearsal Room: Two Dancers*, c. 1871–2.
*Essence* on pink paper.

22.3 × 28.3 cms.
Stamp l.r: Lugt 658.
Vente III, no. 395ii.
Rotterdam, Boymans-van Beuningen Museum.

**41** *Dancers Backstage*, 1872.
Oil on canvas.
24.2 × 18.8 cms.
Signed u.r: 'Degas'.
L. 1024.
Washington, National Gallery of Art, Ailsa Mellon Bruce Collection.

**42** *Ballet Dancer with arms crossed*, 1872.
Oil on canvas.
61.4 × 50.5 cms.
Stamp l.l: Lugt 658.
L. 1025.
Boston, Mass., Museum of Fine Arts, Bequest of John T. Spaulding.

**43** *Dancer adjusting her Shoulder Strap*, c. 1873–4.
*Essence* on pink board.
41.5 × 18 cms.
Stamp l.l: Lugt 658.
Vente III, no. 212 (with two other studies of dancers).
Switzerland, private collection.

**44** *The Rehearsal*, 1873–4.
Oil on canvas.
58.4 × 83.8 cms.
Signed l.l: 'Degas'.
L. 430.
The Burrell Collection, Glasgow Museums and Art Galleries.

**45** *The Dancer Jules Perrot*, c. 1874–5.
Charcoal and black chalk, heightened with white, on pinkish paper.
48.4 × 30.5 cms.
Inscr. u.r: '*reflets rouge fade/lueur dans le cou/pantalon bleu/flanelle/tête rose*'.
Stamp l.l: Lugt 658.
Vente III, no. 157ii.
The Syndics of the Fitzwilliam Museum, Cambridge.

**46** *Two Dancers on Stage,* c.1874.
Oil on paper mounted on panel.
16.8 × 21.8 cms.
Signed u.r: 'Degas'.
USA, private collection.

**47** Study for *Two Dancers at the Bar: Dancer from behind,* c.1876–7.
Black chalk.
31.1 × 20 cms.
Stamp l.l: Lugt 658.
Vente III, no.133iv.
Paris, Musée du Louvre, Département des Arts Graphiques.

**48** Study for *Two Dancers at the Bar,* c.1876–7.
*Essence* on green prepared paper.
47 × 62.5 cms.
Signed l.r: 'Degas'.
L.409.
London, British Museum, Department of Prints and Drawings.

**49** Study for *Two Dancers at the Bar,* c.1876–7.
Pencil, with marks in *essence.*
30.9 × 19.5 cms.
Stamp l.r: Lugt 657.
New York, Mr and Mrs William R. Acquavella.

**50** *Race Horses,* c.1875–8.
Oil on panel.
32.5 × 40.5 cms.
Signed l.l: 'Degas'.
L.387.
Private collection.

**51** *Carlo Pellegrini,* c.1876–7.
*Essence,* watercolour and pastel.
63.2 × 34 cms.
Inscr. l.l: 'à lui/Degas'.
L.407.
London, The Trustees of the Tate Gallery.

**52** *Portrait of a Woman,* c.1876–8.
Monotype, thinned with turpentine, laid down.
21.5 × 16 cms.
Stamp verso: Lugt 657.

140

J.238.
The Art Institute of Chicago, Mrs Potter Palmer Memorial Fund.

**53** *Mlle Bécat aux Ambassadeurs,* c.1875–7.
Oil on tile.
20.3 × 20.3 cms.
Signed on verso: 'Degas'.
L.Suppl. 70.
Private collection.

**54** *Café-concert Singer,* c.1876–7.
Crayon lithograph.
25.2 × 19.2 cms.
Signed on stone l.r: 'Degas'.
RS. 26/i.
London, British Museum, Department of Prints and Drawings.

**55** *Mlle Bécat at the Café-concert des Ambassadeurs,* c.1877–8.
Lithograph.
20.5 × 19.3 cms (image).
RS. 31.
Bern, E.W. Kornfeld.

**56** *Mlle Bécat at the Café-concert des Ambassadeurs: Three Motifs,* c.1877–8.
Lithograph transferred from three monotypes.
29.1 × 24.3 cms (image).
RS. 30.
Bern, E.W. Kornfeld.

**57** Fan: *Dancers and Stage Scenery,* c.1878–9.
Gouache, with gold highlights, on silk.
31 × 61 cms.
Signed u.l: 'Degas'.
L. 556.
Bern, E.W. Kornfeld.

**58** *Laundresses Carrying their Linen in Town,* c.1878–9.
*Essence* on paper mounted on canvas.
46 × 61 cms.
Signed l.r: 'Degas'.
L.410.

Private collection.

**59** *Les Amateurs (Paul Lafond and Alphonse Cherfils examining a Painting),* c.1878–80.
Oil on panel.
28 × 36 cms.
Inscr. u.l: 'Degas/a mes chers amis'.
L. 647.
The Cleveland Museum of Art, Leonard C. Hanna, Jr Collection.

**60** Study for *Diego Martelli,* 1879.
Pencil on page removed from notebook 31.
11.1 × 16.7 cms.
Verso: sketch of man's head and shoulders.
Edinburgh, National Gallery of Scotland.

**61** Study for *Diego Martelli,* 1879.
Black chalk, heightened with white, on yellow-beige paper; squared for transfer.
45 × 29 cms.
Inscr. u.r: 'chez Martelli/3 Avril 79/Degas'.
Vente I, no. 326.
England, private collection.

**62** Study for *Miss Lala at the Circus Fernando,* 1879.
Oil and pastel on canvas.
89 × 39.5 cms.
Stamp on stretcher: Lugt 657.
L.Suppl. 79.
New York, Pierre Matisse.

**63** *At the Louvre: the Etruscan Sarcophagus,* c.1879.
Pencil on page removed from notebook 31.
10.5 × 16.5 cms.
Stamp l.l: Lugt 658.
Williamstown, Mass., Sterling and Francine Clark Art Institute.

**64** *Mary Cassatt at the Louvre: The Etruscan Gallery,* c.1879–80.
Softground etching, drypoint, aquatint and etching.

26.7 × 23.2 cms (platemark).
RS. 51/v.
Rotterdam, Boymans-van Beuningen Museum.

**65** *The Dancing Master Jules Perrot,* c.1880.
Black and brown chalk.
49.5 × 33.2 cms.
Inscr. u.r: 'le danseur Perrot'.
Stamp l.l: Lugt 658.
Vente III, no. 157iii.
Mr David Daniels.

**66** *The Conversation (Ludovic Halévy and Mme Cardinal),* c.1880.
Monotype.
21.3 × 16 cms (image).
Stamp l.r: Lugt 658.
J.46.
The Cleveland Museum of Art, Gift of the Print Club in honour of Henry Sayles Francis.

**67** *Ludovic Halévy and Mme Cardinal,* c.1880.
Pastel over monotype, touched with black chalk.
21.3 × 16 cms (image).
Stamp l.r: Lugt 658.
J.212.
Stuttgart, Staatsgalerie, Graphische Sammlung.

**68** Studies for *Little Dancer of Fourteen Years,* c.1878–80.
Charcoal, heightened with white chalk, on grey paper.
48 × 63 cms.
Stamp l.l: Lugt 658.
Vente III, no. 386.
Private collection.

**69** Nude Study for *Little Dancer of Fourteen Years,* c.1878–80.
Bronze.
Height: 71.8 cms (including base).
Stamp on base: Lugt 658.
Rewald XIX.
Edinburgh, National Gallery of Scotland.

**70** Studies for *Little Dancer of Fourteen Years,* c.1878–80.

Black and brown chalk and pastel, worked with a brush, on grey paper.
47.2 × 58.8 cms.
Stamp l.l: Lugt 658.
Vente III, no. 277.
London, private collection.

**71** Studies for *Little Dancer of Fourteen Years*, c.1878–80.
Pencil, charcoal and pastel on green paper.
48.5 × 30.5 cms.
Stamp l.l: Lugt 658.
Vente III, no. 149.
Thomas Gibson Fine Art Limited.

**72** *Little Dancer of Fourteen Years*, c.1878–81.
Bronze, with pigmented tarlatan skirt and dyed silk bow.
Height: 99.1 cms.
Stamp on base: Lugt 658.
Rewald XX.
University of East Anglia, Robert and Lisa Sainsbury Collection.

**73** *The Washbasin (La Cuvette)*, c.1880–3.
Monotype.
27.7 × 31.2 cms.
J.177.
The Syndics of the Fitzwilliam Museum, Cambridge.

**74** *Study of a Nude Woman drying herself with a Towel*, c.1880–3.
Pencil, heightened with white, on green/grey paper (discoloured; formerly bright blue).
44.6 × 27.9 cms.
Stamp l.l: Lugt 658.
The Visitors of the Ashmolean Museum, Oxford.

**75** *Dancers in the Rehearsal Room, with a Double Bass*, c.1879–85.
Oil on canvas.
39 × 89.5 cms.
Signed l.l: 'Degas'.
L.905.
New York, The Metropolitan Museum of Art, Bequest of Mrs H.O. Havemeyer, 1929, the

H.O. Havemeyer Collection.

**76** *Dancer adjusting her Slipper*, c.1880–5.
Pastel and charcoal on brown paper.
49 × 62 cms.
Signed l.r: 'Degas'.
L.1069.
British Rail Pension Fund Works of Art Collection.

**77** *Dancer adjusting her Tights*, c.1880–5.
Black chalk, heightened with white, over pencil; squared for transfer.
24.2 × 31.3 cms.
Signed l.r: 'Degas'.
Vente III, no. 109d.
The Syndics of the Fitzwilliam Museum, Cambridge.

**78** *Horse and Jockey (The End of the Race)*, c.1883–5.
Black chalk on tracing paper; squared for transfer.
14.7 × 19.8 cms.
Stamp l.l: Lugt 658.
Vente III, no. 354i.
The Burrell Collection, Glasgow Museums and Art Galleries.

**79** *Horse with Lowered Head (Cheval faisant une descente de main)*, c.1883–90.
Bronze.
Height: 18.1 cms.
Stamp on base: Lugt 658.
Rewald XII.
The Syndics of the Fitzwilliam Museum, Cambridge.

**80** *Portrait of a Seated Woman*, c.1885.
Pastel and charcoal on buff paper.
63.8 × 49.5 cms.
Stamp l.l: Lugt 658.
L.1140.
University of Manchester, Whitworth Art Gallery.

**81** *Race-horse and Jockey*, c.1887–90.
Red chalk.

28.3 × 41.8 cms.
Stamp l.l: Lugt 658.
Vente III, no. 130a.
Rotterdam, Boymans-van Beuningen Museum.

**82** *Degas and Zoé Closier*, c.1890–5.
Photograph.
Paris, Bibliothèque Nationale.

**83** *Landscape: Steep Coast*, c.1890–2.
Pastel.
42 × 55 cms.
Signed l.r: 'Degas'.
Geneva, Galerie Jan Krugier.

**84** *Nude Woman standing, drying herself*, c.1891–2.
Lithograph, transfer from monotype, crayon, tusche and scraping.
31 × 19.5 cms (image).
RS.61/ii.
London, British Museum, Department of Prints and Drawings.

**85** *After the Bath*, c.1891–2.
Charcoal on tracing paper, laid down.
35.2 × 25.1 cms.
Stamp l.l: Lugt 658. Verso: Lugt 657.
Vente III, no. 327a.
Williamstown, Mass., Sterling and Francine Clark Art Institute.

**86** *Nude Woman standing, drying herself*, c.1891–2.
Lithograph, transfer from monotype, crayon, tusche and scraping.
33 × 23.5 cms (image).
RS.61/vi.
Cambridge, Mass., Fogg Art Museum, Bequest of Meta and Paul J. Sachs.

**87** *After the Bath (large version)*, c.1891–2.
Lithographic crayon and pencil,

with black wash, on Japanese paper.
35 × 32.8 cms.
Stamp l.l: Lugt 658.
RS.66a.
London, British Museum, Department of Prints and Drawings.

**88** Study for the *Portrait of Mlle Salle*, 1893.
Bronze.
Height: 27 cms.
Rewald XXX.
Fridart Foundation.

**89** *Two Dancers, Harlequin and Colombine*, c.1895.
Charcoal on tracing paper.
27.8 × 23 cms (central sheet).
36 × 30 cms (with additional three strips).
Inscr. u.r: 'rajouter 4c à gauche, 2c à droite, 3c en bas'.
Stamp l.l: Lugt 658.
Vente III, no. 265.
Rotterdam, Boymans-van Beuningen Museum.

**90** *Landscape with Mounted Horsemen*, c.1895.
Oil on canvas.
39 × 89 cms.
Stamp l.l: Lugt 658.
L.764.
Mrs John Hay Whitney.

**91** *Dancer at Rest, Hands behind her Back, Right Leg forward*, c.1890–1900.
Bronze.
Height: 44.5 cms.
Stamp on base: Lugt 658.
Rewald XXIII.
London, The Trustees of the Tate Gallery.

**92** *Dancer adjusting her Shoulder Strap*, c.1890–1900.
Bronze.
Height: 35 cms.
Stamp on base: Lugt 658.
Rewald XXV.
Fridart Foundation.

**93** *Grande Arabesque, second time,*
*c.* 1890–1900.
Bronze.
Height: 43 cms.
Stamp on base: Lugt 658.
Rewald XXXVI.
Private collection, on loan to
Birmingham City Museum and
Art Gallery.

**94** *Half-length Female Nude,*
*c.* 1895–1900.
Charcoal, heightened with white,
on tracing paper, laid down.
53 × 38.8 cms.
Stamp l.r: Lugt 658.
Vente III, no. 247.
The Syndics of the Fitzwilliam
Museum, Cambridge.

**95** *Dancer adjusting her Shoulder*
*Strap, c.* 1895–1900.
Charcoal and pastel on grey
paper.
28 × 47 cms.
Stamp l.l: Lugt 658.
L. 1271.
The Burrell Collection, Glasgow
Museums and Art Galleries.

**96** *Half-length Dancer, adjusting*
*her Shoulder Strap, c.* 1895–1900.
Charcoal and pastel on tracing
paper, laid down.
47.5 × 37 cms.
Signed l.r: 'Degas'.
Bremen, Kunsthalle.

**97** *Study of Four Dancers,*
*c.* 1895–1900.
Charcoal and pastel
(counterproof).
45.4 × 64.5 cms.
Stamp verso: Lugt 657.
University of Manchester,
Whitworth Art Gallery.

**98** *Two Dancers in Yellow,*
*c.* 1895–1900.
Pastel.
60 × 42 cms.
Signed l.r: 'Degas'.
L. 1282.
Private collection.

**99** *Female Nude drying her Neck,*
*c.* 1900.
Charcoal on tracing paper, laid
down.
79.3 × 76.2 cms.
Inscr. l.l: 'L8/90v88'.
Stamp l.l: Lugt 658.
Vente III, no. 246.
The Provost and Fellows of
King's College, Cambridge
(Keynes Collection); on loan to
the Fitzwilliam Museum.

**100** *Nude drying her Hair, c.* 1900.
Charcoal and pastel on tracing
paper, laid down.
77 × 75 cms.
Stamp l.l: Lugt 658.
L. 1425.
Lausanne, Musée Cantonal des
Beaux-Arts.

**101** *Nude standing beside a Chair,*
*c.* 1900–5.
Charcoal on tracing paper, laid
down.
91.4 × 66 cms.
Private collection, on loan to the
Fitzwilliam Museum,
Cambridge.

**102** *Three Nude Dancers at Rest,*
*c.* 1900–5.
Lithograph, reworked in black
chalk and pastel.
19.5 × 26.8 cms (platemark).
Stamp: Lugt 657.
RS. 59a.
Bern, E.W. Kornfeld.

**103** *After the Bath, c.* 1905.
Pastel and charcoal on tracing
paper, laid down.
78 × 56 cms.
Stamp l.l: Lugt 658.
L. 1343.
The Columbus Gallery of Fine
Arts, Ferdinand Howald
Collection.

**104** Anon. (Degas ?)
*Three Photographs of Dancers,*
*c.* 1895 or earlier.
Paris, Bibliothèque Nationale.

# Lenders

Mr and Mrs William R. Acquavella 49
Boston, Mass., Museum of Fine Arts 42
Bremen, Kunsthalle 2, 5, 96
Basel, Kunstmuseum, Öffentliche
    Kunstsammlungen 35
British Rail Pension Fund Works of Art
    Collection 76
Cambridge, The Syndics of the Fitzwilliam
    Museum 7, 8, 28, 29, 45, 73, 77, 79, 94
    The Provost and Fellows of King's College 99
Cambridge, Mass., Fogg Art Museum 12, 20, 31
    86
The Art Institute of Chicago 24, 33, 52
The Cleveland Museum of Art 10, 30, 59, 66
The Columbus Gallery of Fine Arts 103
Mr David Daniels 32, 65
Detroit Institute of Arts 17
University of East Anglia, Robert and Lisa
    Sainsbury Collection 72
Edinburgh, National Gallery of Scotland 60, 69
Marianne Feilchenfeldt 3, 11, 14
Fridart Foundation 88, 92
Geneva, Galerie Jan Krugier 83
Thomas Gibson Fine Art Limited 71
Glasgow Museums and Art Galleries, The Burrell
    Collection 34, 44, 78, 95
Kasmin Ltd 37
E. W. Kornfeld 55, 56, 57, 102
Lausanne, Musée Cantonal des Beaux-Arts 100
London, British Museum, Department of Prints
    and Drawings 48, 54, 84, 87
    The Trustees of the Tate Gallery 51, 91
University of Manchester, Whitworth Art
    Gallery 80, 97
Pierre Matisse 62

New York, The Metropolitan Museum of Art,
    H.O. Havemeyer Collection 75
The Metropolitan Museum of Art, Lehman
    Collection 18, 19
Oxford, The Visitors of the Ashmolean Museum
    1, 74
Paris, Bibliothèque Nationale 82
    Musée du Louvre, Département des Arts
    Graphiques 25, 39, 47
    Musée Gustave Moreau 15
Rotterdam, Boymans-van Beuningen Museum
    26, 40, 64, 81, 89
Stuttgart, Staatsgalerie, Graphische Sammlung
    67
Toledo Museum of Art 21
Tours, Musée des Beaux-Arts 36
Washington, Dumbarton Oaks Research Library
    and Collection 38
    National Gallery of Art 41
Mrs John Hay Whitney 90
Williamstown, Mass., Sterling and Francine
    Clark Art Institute 4, 6, 9, 16, 63, 85
Zurich, Kunsthaus (on loan) 13
Private Collections 22, 23, 27, 43, 46, 50, 53, 58,
    61, 68, 70, 93, 98, 101

## Photographic credits

Archivi Alinari 10, 62, 91; A.C. Cooper 35;
Prudence Cumming 20, 98, 107; T. Eddie and
D. Graham 70; Lauros-Giraudon 6, 42; Musées
Nationaux, Paris 5, 22, 38, 43, 60, 61, 63, 66, 76,
80, 106, 127, 148, 151, 163; Marie-Louise Pérony
34; Eric Pollitzer 119; Tom Scott 110; John Webb
27, 157